World Voice:

Speaking Our Truth

Publisher: Santiago, Inc.
224 Post Rd STE #4 -182
Westerly, RI 02891

ISBN 978-1-937526-00-9

Library of Congress Control Number: 2011912395

Disclaimer

Some of the events in this book are based on true events, however, they have been fictionalized and all persons appearing in this work are fictitious. Any resemblances to real people, living or dead, are coincidental.

The publisher accepts no liability for the content of this book, or for the consequences of any actions taken on the basis of the information provided. You are notified that disclosing, copying, distributing or taking any action in reliance on the contents of this information is strictly prohibited.

By proceeding further than this statement, you agree not to hold the author, publisher or any of the book's sponsors responsible for anything you do, read, write, or think from reading this book. The publisher believes you should be of legal age to read this book, and in the USA that age is 18 years old.

The opinions in the stories, poems, or other writing do not necessarily reflect the beliefs, thoughts or views of the authors or the publisher.

For many authors in this book English is not their mother tongue so we (the editors) ask you keep an open and uncritical mind when finding a word choice or sentence structure that may be different than how you would say it. Deliberation and consideration has been used in deciding what to edit and what to leave as a mark of the author's voice.

If you submitted writings that did not make it into this version of the book, your pieces are still in the World Voice Archive and will be considered for the next book. For more information please email JosephS@Santiago-inc.com.

! ATTENTION ALL WRITERS !

HERE IS YOUR CHANCE TO PUBLISH YOUR WORK IN AN ONGOING SERIES OF
BOOKS CALLED
WORLD VOICE

***

WE ARE LOOKING FOR EXPERIENCED AND
AMATEUR WRITERS. THE AIM OF THIS PROJECT IS TO CONTINUE A WRITTEN
EXPRESSION OF WHAT IS FUNDAMENTALLY IMPORTANT TO PEOPLE ALL
AROUND THE WORLD.
*
***

SHARE YOUR STORY.

***

WRITE ABOUT YOUR LIFE.

***

WHAT REALLY MATTERS TO YOU?

***

HAVE A PERSONAL JOURNAL? SUBMIT IT!

***

Examples of submissions are essays, poetry, biographies, creative writings, photographs of your original art, and photographs.

Please go to http://worldvoiceproject.com and click on **Online Submission** to submit your works.

To check out books published under the World Voice theme go to www.Amazon.com and search for World Voice: Inspiring a Conscious Signature ISBN: 9780578050256.

Be a sponsor of the next World Voice book!

Your ad will circulate the globe with each book sold, showcasing your company and its advertisement as the sponsor. For more information on becoming a sponsor write to josephs@santiago-inc.com and put **Sponsor Inquiry** in the subject line.

Other products by Joseph A Santiago and Santiago, Inc.
World Voice: Beginnings
World Voice: Invisible Lines
World Voice: Connected Communities
World Voice: Inspiring a Conscious Signature
My Post Bush American Life (Audio Series)
Mindfulness and Peaceful Living (Limited Run)
The Hypnotic Regression of Mr. Strawberry (Audio & Video)
Stop Smoking Now (Audio)
Lose Weight Now (Audio)
Speaking out: Sexuality and Rhode Island's Pride (Audio)

national coalition for sexual freedom

The NCSF is committed to creating a political, legal and social environment in the US that advances equal rights for consenting adults who engage in alternative sexual and relationship expressions.

We pursue our vision through direct services, education, advocacy, and outreach, in conjunction with our partners, to directly benefit these communities.

https://ncsfreedom.org/

NCSF
822 Guilford Avenue
Box 127
Baltimore, Maryland
21202-3707
(410) 539-4824
ncsfreedom@ncsfreedom.org

DO NO HARM

DO NO HARM is the effort of a circle of friends to make the world a kinder and gentler place.

We have no ties to any organization or religion. **DO NO HARM** is a non-profit non-organization.

If you think you're a **member**,

You're a **member**.

If you think you're not a **member**,

You're an honorary **member**.

Please help us promote this simple message.

Visit <u>www.donoharm.us</u> for more details and for free **DO NO HARM** bumper stickers, wrist bands, and round decals.

Photo Time Capsule

DISCLAIMER

. POETRY .

POETRY BY *ALI ABDOLREZAEI - TRANSLATED BY ABOL FROUSHAN*   **2**
  An Oak
  Help!
  Moonface
  Paris in Renault
  Tehran
POETRY BY *GALE EATON*   **12**
  At the Fellowship Hour
POETRY BY *JASMINE ADAMS*   **14**
  Reality
  Sick...
POETRY BY *JILLIAN CHASE*   **16**
  The Bloody Cry
  Some Kind of Wonderful
POETRY BY *JOHN LAWRENCE*   **17**
  Untitled
POETRY BY *JOSEPH SANTIAGO*   **18**
  A Walk in the Woods
POETRY BY *KOLBY ANDRADE*   **19**
  Blinded
  Change
  Chemical Reaction
  Earthquake
  The gift of special gifts
  Happily Ever After?
  Just Deal
  Pretty Little Mess
  Silence
  Stone
  Things Gathered
  Thinkable
  The World
POETRY BY *MATTHEW SCOTT HARRIS*   **25**
  Grievance of Misspent Youth!
  This Lonely Middle-aged Man!
  Extraordinary Pillars of These United States!
POETRY BY *MORGAN COTTRELL*   **28**
  A Fall Day With Giggling Girl
POETRY BY *RILEY DAVIS*   **29**
  Blind

    Distance
    Time Watchers
POETRY BY THUPTEN TENDHAR   **31**
    Help Me Create a New World
POETRY BY RICHARD V. TRAVISANO   **34**
    In Spain
    Light
    Listen
    Middlebridge Nights
    On Re-meeting a Friend After a Decade [Does Lightning Strike Twice?]
    Pennies From Heaven
    Southern Spain Bus Trip: Huelva to Sevilla
    Where Are The Mae Wests?

SHORT . STORIES .   **40**
    ANGELA'S SHAME   **41**
      By Richard Muto
    BIRTHDAY BREAKDOWN   **45**
      By Melissa Toni
    CLIFF WALKER   **49**
      By Riley Davis
    CREATION MYTH   **51**
      By Matthew Silva
    DANCING WITH MOUNT WASHINGTON   **55**
      By John Lawrence
    ESCAPE   **58**
      By Carrie Anne Perez
    EVADE RESPONSIBILITY   **66**
      By Riley Davis
    FAMILIAR AMBIGUITY   **68**
      By Joseph A. Santiago
    FRUSTRATION   **70**
      By Joseph A. Santiago
    INJECTION   **72**
      By Riley Davis
    THE LADIES   **73**
      By Richard Muto
    LOST AND FOUND   **84**
      By Alex Dobrenko
    THE NIGHT SHIFT   **88**
      By Richard V. Travisano
    PRECAMBRIAN PREDECESSORS   **89**
      By Matthew Scott Harris
    THE RAVEN AND THE SPARROW   **95**

By Alexandra Epervary
SASHA VS. THE RED VESTS   97
By Alex Dobrenko
SAUSAGES   103
By Ali Abdolrezaei – Translated By Abol Froushan
SKY BLUE   104
By Alexandra Epervary
SNAPSHOTS OF OUR FAMILY TRIP TO ARUBA   106
By Melissa Toni
VISION   122
By Joseph A. Santiago

ESSAYS, MUSINGS, MEMOIRS, AND EVERYTHING ELSE
A MAYAN EXPERIENCE: A URI PHYSICAL THERAPY STUDENT SERVICE-LEARNING
PROJECT IN GUATEMALA   127
By Jennifer Audette
A SMALL STONE OF WONDER   145
By Joseph A. Santiago
A STORY OF UN   147
By Joseph A.Santiago
EMPTINESS IS NOT A BOX   149
By Joseph A. Santiago
IMPOSSIBLE TO RETURN HOME   151
By Matthew Scott Harris
INTROSPECTION IS A BEAR   155
By Joseph A. Santiago
MONOLOGUE NUMBER ONE   156
By Matthew Scott Harris
MY STORY OF MENTAL HEALTH AND MINDFULNESS   158
By Chelsea Longa
SNAKE: A CHRISTMAS SHOPPING STORY   162
By Gale Eaton
SPEAKING TO MY FUTURE SELF   164
By Joseph A. Santiago
SURFACING MUSIC   165
By Joseph A. Santiago
THE COST OF ANGER   166
By Alexandra Epervary
THE INCONCEIVABLE FINISH   168
By Michael Cichowicz
THE RIVER   176
By Riley Davis
TRADITIONAL FAMILY CULTURE: MONO VS. POLY POLITICAL FAMILY PERSPECTIVE   177

By Joseph A. Santiago
LIFE BY ASSOCIATION   **181**
By Joseph Santiago

CLOSING   **188**
SANTIAGO INC. COMPANY PROFILE   **189**

Photography By Riley Davis

∎ Poetry ∎

An Oak

On your death darling tears are too little.

They promised me
        promised me you'll rise as an oak.

An oak
        by a little brook
        that gets deeper as it goes
        as it widens to a stream
        a stream that renders its rivery water
        to the young deer resting in your shade.

Promise me you won't be jealous
        'cause sooner or later
        I'll be a river right by your side.

By Ali Abdolrezaei

Help!

Even the Lady Sea
in the most southerly place of Sir Spain
that's an enclave of blues and water

is a tubful of cooking oil
poured into a pan and vertical sunshine

is a hipster fire
that fries people busy bathing.

I wouldn't trust the camaraderie of
such watery hands

Like a flared pair of jokers
support is a distant hand
that appeared out of an empty grave
and is beckoning still.

By Ali Abdolrezaei

Moonface

She so surrounded me and I so gathered her up in me
that she's no longer around.
Don't know where her bosom's gone.
Tonight is flat-chested
and in order to die
I need her eminent grace Miss Sentiment .

I'm shaven
       to have an eye to eye with you
       why aren't you there?

Taxis no longer take my solitude, I stay behind
'till something comes to make me a quiet place
       like a camel in the desert
       an old tortoise on the plain
       or like the plane in a London sky
       in which I can fly --but where?

Like yesterday's rain urged me to buy this umbrella
or this snow that came down after the rain
and sent me out of the house.
Give me a ring.
Do something.
You're not snow so I could melt you
you're not rain so you can could wet me
you're a brush fire
       that turns all to cinder and moves on.

By Ali Abdolrezaei

Paris in Renault

Out of the blue past so many deaths we were born mad!
How would we know the mirror forgets whatever it sees
we believed the wind gets through the chinks in walls
how would we know the wind stays behind a closed door.
Senselessly past so many deaths we are a graveyard so wide across
we U-turn only a hop away from our destination.
We weave in and out of outdistancing one another

To how many more margins does our distance stretch?

This damned hooha rising from which neighborhood window
which damned ear does it corner in
and which clock hand does it revolve around?
This very tomorrow which rained a remote smile on our lips
heads in which direction of the wind?
Shall I stand to say Seven?

I'm such a weeping willow for all this withstanding the wind unswayed
that in the whereabouts of the hand on the clock
worn-out by this coming and going of all the Sevens, I'm spent.
What town calls its travelers back? Which road?

I swear in the name of the water that drips from our hands
I won't shrink from wanting you.
You just write Death all over my letters; yet, I will live!

Mr! Hey Taxi! Tour of all Isfahan for a thousand!
I threw thirty hearts to the sea
 to keep three arches for lovers on Khaju bridge.
Madam! I'm not afraid of the police.
I can raise havoc and dream.
 A long pavement crowds on the main street
rioting in dreamy love making.
At times fear is a lecherous mayor
who parks his mistress.
Sir! I can move from this house too
become the sidled dream of walls
and be no gypsy lover.

I won't blame the moon for the distance
that this rain has brought the sea to my side
(a saying that speaks like a poem)
or the youth I left behind on a bicycle.
I won't blame the moon for distance
when there was no way through.
You so short cut that Saturday
it poured down from my calendar.

There are only two paths ahead
I won't take the third.

I am woebegone at the foot of the poem I am writing

I should just say "I love you" and die.
These days star means the ultimate woman who's coming.

The kite was only a lifelong captive in my hands.
A man who with a kiss on a hand calls an old city
a man who walked on his weeping
slept in the dream of your eyes.
I am far enough from the sea to be a heretic for you
sit in my eyes and pray at the bottom of the sea.
These days star means the ultimate woman who comes
after her 'bird's a goner' poem
like an apple living on a tree I am wonder struck
and don't know what I mean.

Roads arrive from town to town
bridges from highway to parallel highway
why don't we arrive anywhere?
Still the mirror jails an unnamable
that is everyone's loneliness.
Still everywhere there's a road for me to traverse
no pedestrian is the last one alone
no pedestrian practiced the man
no pedestrian ever asked "Hey Mister?"
And my spouse wept last night
for the coffee house that died under water
for the sea embracing the houses last night.
I saw the Sea of Chamkhalee in my notebook and crossed it out
the poem is not like the poet
each night wanting a new bosom
you want to let me go?
you think I'll die of grief?
I'll go North, and never mind the girls who don't rhyme.

Ding! Dong!

Who is it?

It's the Milkman, O the Milkman!

Sorry! I have no child to get more milk for
no name to peddle around town
for all the gauges gaping at I Know Not What

when do we arrive anywhere?

There where we arrive may be not where you are
for one night that hasn't gone in my empty arms stay with me.
I'll be spending my days knocking around the margins
following our fallen-in-love ever toward you.
Even though I hear no wailing
say a word and I'll become the song of the reed.
I wish the sky had a heart and would tear away from me
I wish it hinted at when we'll be feathered together
As it is, I'd sooner not have picked from desire's bunch of grapes
and wouldn't have said this bottle shall be wine.
I said hey, bring back my furthest desire.
What shall I do it didn't work out, will I be yours? Hey?
I wanted to offer you so much heart --
Hell it didn't work out, I'll fall in love with another.

Not much time was left to the conversation of the cockerels

I said: "Right

I can't sleep again"

I said: "Right

They must have gagged the cockerels"

I said: "Right"

I had to tell you Good bye!

As I was saying "rights" he hung up.

I'm standing next to the door
the architecture of your body is etched
on the bed in the corner of the floor
I keep puffing and staring at the clothes tree
trouser legs from behind whose stripes a bird flew
I wish I clipped its wings forever..

Where are you carrying these days?
Whatever there was in the mirror, the pictures intimated.
How can I find all sevens in the mirror?

How many more margins does our distance stretch?
How many more seconds-- Ha?

You pounded the sea on the opposite wall
so I sit and watch the extravagance of youth on my face?
Just two clock hands till dawn can I stay in the corner of the square,
Where are your windows?

Next to a man turning the pages of history
I flew a glimpse to the skies and said how blue are your eyes!
But my bird was not always blue.
Only our faces see the mirror and through the chink of a wall a woman.
Those days my thoughts strolled through the windows of the room
and paused so long on the tree opposite
that autumn was beckoned to fall in the village
and breaking
kept calibrating the wind on my wings.

I arrived late for a lifetime
like all the benches in the park
that were installed for the falling leaves.
I'm sick of all this.
Which road's pebble broke this window?
Who is the one over my head who left?
They put a night on day and say
Yesterday left, today passed away, what do you do tomorrow?
Sometimes I have died a thousand-fold
sometimes I have torn God apart.
I've lost you in your own very eyes
like the neon death of
MIRROR MAN of Armani Street
MIRROR MA of A ma i treet
MI ROR MA omaneet
MI OR MA ma et
I OR A ma t
I O A ma t
I O A m
I
                        zzz zapped out...

Water has brought a mirror to watch

the sound of my skin and the alleys
that open out a window on my brow.
Gossip dropped in on a sitting of the women of the alley
whose doors had sunset
and gave autumn away to the branches
simply to take you away from me.
I have not trampled the yellow of all the leaves
to ask your forgiveness.
The pomegranate that was shelved on the branch
never went hunting for suitors.
They put a guitar in my hand and a rendezvous for never
they strolled around in my eyes
snatched all pictures in the mirror
and never noticed this branch doesn't give a step to the sky.

Always, I know, the one who slips goes all the way
to the bottom of the precipice
nevertheless whatever I see in the mirror, is still me.
Take a handful of water and tell my face what secret it has to tell
the pomegranate that is toothless!
If it weren't for the trees, how would you see autumn?
If spring left, how would neighborhood apples turn red?
I know the one who says 'I love you' has snatched all the apples
otherwise all these stones are the only excuse
for the window's broken smile.

The sound that rushed through the reed has brought me here to you!
For you to come back from the most closed window
 and sit at my table
and let that debauched flame which fired the wing of the moth
come to put a fire on the logs and the alley
to be the haunting ground of so many cockerels.
So people see me falling asleep behind a door to say "you!"
A you who would say behind every window
"There is at times a closed window."
Why closed again?
Sometimes all the clock hands arrive
so you return
and on the side of a street which dawns next to tomorrow
be the green light just for me.
If you come back
I'll take that far holy city as my birthplace
'cause you are more beautiful and just

as grand as the dome of the mosque
and you're these carpet flowers
and these eyes that flower on road sides.

Strolling in the summer of Chamkhalee,
Is that your hair on my shoulder or is it raining?
If you come back I won't kill myself
(but if you don't I won't do that either).

Every year, like the other girls who come, she goes.
I thought, "Just write - You... "
the rest is just the murmur of the rain.
Sometimes when drop by drop it puts fingers on your shoulder
it wants you to come back and take the sea
that has fallen by the wayside
these very circles of the rain that reach each other
on the water and hold hands.

--"Hello," that means you're a poet?

--If you take fewer than two steps, there is a house I have.

--The rain weeps berries in your garden

--No one says "Yes" twice!

Coolies run around to pick the next load and die empty.
Our lives that are passing are not past
if you walk even death won't reach us.
Always the one who wants without permission
loses without permission .
So you alone watch whatever tears I bring
then write "Death" all over my letters

I shall live.

Without a vase for a lifetime
I have poured a river out of the sea in my backyard
I am bored with the sea surrounding me and the Caspian's plea,
how can I return to Tehran where I've left myself behind?
No longer will I go back to those days of Langrude

(a hot and humid climate suits death).
I adore Tehran of Friday's parks, should I return?
Fallen into the tea cup and the spoon's wake
my eyes keep swaying in and out of you.
So stir together sugar, water and wine
they form an accent for all the fantasies I have for you.
You're so cold and cruel you drink up the walls
not knowing the mirror doesn't forget its glimpses.
When I think of you, I let the window embrace me
and wipe the moon with a cloth
that sucks the dust off our pictures.
I take no umbrella there nor wear a hat
the rain is just me who comes sobbing
not wine but end to end water.
I'm so brimming full my bottle's overflowing
this falling over myself has crests like the sea
but I don't know which hand's throw is upon you.
When will I be calmed to pal around?
But my bent branch was not immune
from the thrown ravages of stone.

You the sun, and me the earth, lived like a lone moth afire
and so many burning moth wings paid for my glowing desire.
 How can I put a guard at the door of the house I have not?
The red of which branch was it that drove me mad?
How can I travel the fruitfully
through a town that inherited nothing?
I am but feathers battered by so much wind
that I have lost my canary wings.
I'm the dashed lines of a rain not inclined to fall out of your sight.
I am gone from myself like a wave on a beach.

Like wave upon wave of the sea
I am falling in upon myself.

By Ali Abdolrezaei

Tehran

This café is fine.	Right!
Has great coffee	Agreed!
Blue sky above.	Fine!

Not blind darling
I can see beautiful chairs round such a table
I don't deny the seaside music
and after this coffee
        these fulsome lips delectably waiting
and I know well how to swim in the air of this unknowing
I know how to see through this I know not what.

I know!
Sitting so comfortably in your eyes
whichever side I reach
I can take a bit of you even more delectable
I'm not stupid
I understand you're right .   OK!

But if all this
and everything was under the blackened sky of Tehran
we'd have been so much in place

By Ali Abdolrezaei

[All of Ali Abdolrezaei's poems are translated from Persian into English and he has chosen to include his address and welcomes correspondence.

Abol Froushan
47 Cathcart Road
Chelsea, London
United Kingdom
SW10 9JE]

Poetry by Gale Eaton

At the Fellowship Hour

Old now --
        repeating yourself,
        casting with the same frayed words
        after years too slippery to hold --
you tell me again
        how much your father, fool
                and overgenerous,
                lost when you were three;
how hard your mother worked,
        and you too;
how the judge made your false accuser
        that white woman, pay your wages,
        and let you go.
Nobody knows, you say again;
nobody knows what this old black skin
has seen.

Sitting beside you on the lumpy couch,
I ask what happened then.

I could write a book, you say.
Minister tell me, Gertrude,
you could write a book.

Your eyes, ringed blue and pale
as water, glance at me
slanted as your words;
the secret playing at your lips
repeats for a moment

a child's failed poker face.

You are part Swedish, but
        they wouldn't let you
        spell your name that way;
        wasn't fit for colored.
Whites don't know, you tell me;

whites forget, but Jesus
was the color of the earth.

Tell me again this week, stories
worn smooth now as rosaries
or worry stones; stories
too few, too small, to
wall back time much longer.

I was with my mother, you say;
with her at the last. I never left her.
She didn't die alone.
It meant a
lot.

You peer into my face
for what it ought to mean.
You are a child now
and need her with you.
Strangers do nothing to make up for it.
I give you the occasional meal,
can't often bring myself to kiss you, and
however much it hurts, I always leave
too soon.

By Gale Eaton

Poetry by Jasmine Adams

Reality

Born into an alcoholic and drug abusing family...
      Grew up in a lonely and argumentative household...
            Raised by my brother...Life has taken its toll on me.
                  Me and Life alone......have war.

My methods for love are somewhat unorganized, and I'm tired of being stuck,
Body after body...
      Countless kisses and touches...
            Too much of it can make you feel like...
                  You're no longer worth waiting for.

You desperately search for someone to blame,
Immediately letting your mind begin the exhausted cycle of reminiscence.
Past relationships come to mind as you silently file names into categories...
....And then you realize who *is* the main one to blame...**the donor**!

The donor is the one to blame, for this dosage of disabled emotions,
The one to accuse for my personal disobedience...and mental instability,
The reason for my neediness for a careless man to love whole-heartedly...

The reason for so many decisions in my past...

By Jasmine Adams

Sick...

I'm turning into my mother...
      ...constantly needing **distractions to preoccupy my mind from**
questioning, wondering... what you doin'...who you with and where you
goin'?

Not sure if I'm getting sick of listening to that voice that's telling me it's **worth**
it to continue to give you all of me.

I need to hide from attachment...because the way that God's tellin' me how
I'm gone end up...is haunting me...

...scaring me...
...making me...
...think so much more than you're used to seeing.

But I can't help it...you showed me love after I proved myself to you a million times...
...I guess my work is almost done...
...I just gotta prove myself a million more.

'Til you notice that I'm the one God sent for you...
...And now you're not sure whether or not to try a "return to sender" or just deal with the monthly payments.

This shit hurts...
...I need answers...
...Do you love me or not...?
...Do you want me or not...?
Are you thinkin' maybe we're
better off as just friends?

I'm tired of playing this guessing game.

You see...I done had the "ballin' type that called all night, keep claiming he coming through...
I had the CEO that would bring me dough cause he always had something to prove...
I had the so called God-Man...who thought he could do everything God can....so he was closer to God than the church-man...
I had the 'meet me at the poetry spot' down to earth man...
I had the nikka from the club who was only good for a fuck, and I had a street nikka that keep claiming he was down on his luck.
I had a playa, with no goals and no heart...just game...and I had the twenty-four in the studio man....on his way to fame...
I had the control freak who thought that he could keep me on a chain...and I had a nikka that lied so much, I don't even know his real name...

But at the end of the night...they all made me feel the same...
I had a million things to lose... and not a damn thing to gain..."

But you're my other half...look at all we overcame...
I don't want to lose you...cause then I'll lose myself...
(who I am with you...which took so many years to gain.)

By Jasmine Adams

Poetry by Jillian Chase

The Bloody Cry

Tears fall from her cuts
Blood gushes from her eyes
The doctor dilates her skin
The knife slices her tiny pupils
Soft epidermis wrinkles
the iris' s lashes cry

Her hands are fine now
Scars on the eyelid left behind
Thin line of beauty is drawn on her leg
Thin line of eye shadow on her upper lid
Hair of imperfection on her 'perfect' face
Deep gash of jealousy on her retina

(And tears fall from her cuts
blood gushes from her eyes.)

By Jillian Chase

Some Kind of Wonderful

Dew. Drops form.
Light. Sun rises.
Crisp. Cool air.
Run. Through fields.
Flee. From sanity.
Forget. Life's monotony.
Excuse. Past wrongs.
Live. Life fully.
Breathe. In deep.
Set. Sun down.
Dark. No shadows.
Lies. None hidden.
Flowers. Fall asleep.
Dew. Drops form.

Light. Sun rises.
New. All knew.

Poetry by John Lawrence

Untitled

In a snow white sani-chamber next to places far away

I grope within the present for this piece of yesterday

Within which I will oscillate, beyond which I have been

Behind which I must castigate to bring me back again

Without which I am out before tomorrow doesn't sing

The stases of the overture that we can never bring

To bear upon the notion of my own sweet by and by

And the ever-ending motion of my precious alibi

By John Lawrence

Poetry by Joseph Santiago

A Walk in the Woods

In every step I seek to be the wind so that trouble might blow right by me.

In every thought I drink deeply of life so I might be like the sea lapping
at the many creatures it unites even as it reaches out to stroke the shore.

In every action if I were like fire I would burn away the branches of conflict
to take away the sting of sharp edges so they would not consume us.

If my words were like the earth, I would always return to balance,
never fearing the threats of pain, and with loving patience I would bury
conflict by settling in the cracks that trace the imaginary castings of society.

If I were emptiness I would be seen like snow clothing the essences that are
known as the unbounded universe. I would make room for form and variety. I
would welcome change lovingly and begin to explore myself beyond the
dewy outline of what I believed myself to be.

If I were to put all of these things at the mercy of the brooding storm or the
fair kindness of a lazy day, you might still look right over me.

By Joseph A. Santiago

Poetry by Kolby Andrade

Blinded

Now I lay me down to sleep,
I let my conscience slowly seep,
Let the truth bleed deep from my heart for you.
Clearly it's the only way to show you.

Open your eyes.
I'm right here.
I've always been here.
How can you be so blind?

Now I lay me down to sleep,
Forever in your mind, I'll speak,
Whisper thoughts and move mountains for you.
Scream for you.
Until you realize, with your real eyes.
Or are they real lies?
Can you see?

By Kolby Andrade

Change

Change isn't always bitter,
In fact, most of the time it's sweet.
Everyone needs a taste of change.
Wash down your walls of cliché and statistics.
Open your eyes a little.
Take in a little more air.
Exhale a little louder.
And watch the world.

By Kolby Andrade

Chemical Reaction

I watched water change from liquid to ice.
I watched white clouds turn nimbus black.
I watched birds' wings spread and not come back.
Colored flames and toxic air, chemicals mix, chemicals react.

By Kolby Andrade

Earthquake

I'm shaking, not breaking, but this breeze is breath taking.
I'm hanging on, I'm bleeding, and pleading, I swear, I'm hanging on.
The world is being ripped to shreds, the rain is pouring, it may be hailing,
I'm feeling sick, I feel like wailing.

But here I am,
Still standing. not crawling.
Still breathing, I'm defeating.
Not worthless, I'm creating..

I'll stand tall,
Though my world might fall,
I'll watch it rip; I'll watch it shatter; but if I'm still here, all that won't matter.

By Kolby Andrade

The gift of special gifts

I'll give you the key to karma,
Unlock the door to desire.
Take me higher, the desert of doom couldn't get any drier.
Give me the hookah of hope, the heroin of heartache,
The acid of adventure, the taste of your time.
Cherish my chaotic closure. Burn my biggest bridges.
Love what's yours, and love what's mine.

By Kolby Andrade

Happily Ever After?

And so the story goes.
I'm on my way down the highway of happiness,
Letting my spirit shine like the sun,
Down on this pretty mess of a planet which we call earth.

Some days the sun shines, and some days it pours,
Leaving me gasping for air.

I experience love.
I experience heartache.
Then downfall after heartbreak.
Traveling at my own pace.
Too fast is a mistake.
Life could be over in the blink of an eye,
Beauty is around me, just look to the sky.

By Kolby Andrade

Just Deal

I just deal...
Because it's who I am.
I complain about three times a month
(with the exceptions of PMS and mood swings).
I'm not going to claim that I'm depressed, because I don't visit a shrink.
I'm an optimistic pessimist
a walking, talking, breathing oxymoron.
I'm an independent, intelligent young woman.
Who has far too much to say.
For the most part I'm proud of who I'm becoming.
I'm going to put the past on the shelf.
I'm going to smile, laugh, take chances and live.
I'm going to stick my middle finger in the air.
I'm going to say, " Fuck your feelings"
I'm going to live for me.
I just deal...

By Kolby Andrade

Pretty Little Mess

Things get a little messy.
Things get a little fucked up.
Caught in predicaments you don't want.
Beautiful features you fear to flaunt.
Can't let go and you won't give up.
You're my dirty little mistake.
Also my favorite screw-up.

By Kolby Andrade

Silence

Silence!

Is it the absence of sound?
Or is it the presence of truth?
Is it really golden?
Or is it a time for our demons to speak?
Is silence really quiet?
Or is it as loud as it seems?.

By Kolby Andrade

STATE OF MIND

Connected in a way no one understands.
Playing a big role,
In a story unplanned.
Fingers intertwined
Mixed feelings combine.
Not easy to explain,
When love's a state of mind.

By Kolby Andrade

Stone

He spoke the words through parted lips.
His gaze lost in space.
When I raised my eyes to look at him.
I couldn't believe his face.
" Stone." He spoke.
Stone, he saw.

By Kolby Andrade

Things Gathered

I'll give you the key to karma.
Unlock the door of desire.
Take me higher, the desert of doom couldn't get any drier.
Give me the hookah of hope.
The heroin of heartache.
The acid of adventure.
The taste of your time.
Cherish my chaotic closure.
Burn my biggest bridges.
Love what's yours.
And love what's mine.

By Kolby Andrade

Thinkable

If thinking people stopped thinking,
What would they be?

If the thinking did the unthinkable,
What would it mean?

If the thinking stopped thinking,
what would be missed that was meant to be seen?

By Kolby Andrade

The World

The world is such a disastrous place.
It is strange and abnormal.
Yet wondrous and magical.
Beautiful sights fill the world,
Though many hideous sights surface too,
Creating a darker aura for all.

The world is such an imperfect place.
Good and evil woven together.
Creating a marvelous quilt of life.
People weak, and people strong,
Goals created and dreams chased.
Some give up, and some die trying.

The world is a sphere in the eyes of science,
But to humanity, an oddly shaped figure of imagination.
A work of art, an amazing place,.
Filled with mixed emotion.
Spun with diversity, culture, love and war.
The world is worth our fighting for.

By Kolby Andrade

Grievance of Misspent Youth!

woe toward an adolescence
where self-destruction poisoned existence --
emotional, physical, social
and spiritual development.

now at fifty
i bitterly lament
the lost opportunities
of healthy and natural
interpersonal and romantic experiences.

those years of introvesion and withdrawal
left a characteristic imprint on my person.

aloofness, shyness, solitariness
became more prominent with age
and increased alienation
between myself and others.

a future destitute of affection and intimacy
(rather , one marked with despair and loneliness)
presently haunts my psyche.

even the moments of joy and pleasure
tend to be over-shadowed
with gloom and sadness
by this doomed and prophetic fate.

appreciation of the beauty
and magnificence in life and nature
pronounces a longing for another
with whom to gloat and share
these myriad and wondrous marvels.

no! the future
will witness further moments

of distress and gravity
until surrender unto death!

By Matthew Scott Harris

This Lonely Middle-aged Man!

i grieve silently
and hear the echoing reverberation
within the great abyss of my breast.

this somewhat solitary and celibate existence
devoid of mutual affection and love
diminishes the will to live.

engage i must my spirit of hope
and give a friendly gesture
smile to those whom cross my path
with an offbeat chance
to receive a likeness of my deeds.

By Matthew Scott Harris

Extraordinary Pillars of These United States!

George Washington and Abraham Lincoln
epitomized and vocalized special flair
marshaled native talent
in Modus Operandi of bootstraps dare
acquired evanescent reverence
and closest role to God like air!

Now first and sixteenth president
honored on anniversary of their birth
renown places far and wide
over this planet Earth
for courage and strength for American
which spirit touches across
each urban area from home to hearth!

These outsize personas held dream

where fledgling American state
acquired a reputation
home to a country with a winning team!
Among the myth and lore
surrounding each of these great men
their stature grows more and more
these paternal figures
United States can never ignore!

By Matthew Scott Harris

A Fall Day With Giggling Girl

Stepping on acorns just to hear then crack,
Marching forward, and marching back;
You face the wind, and close your eyes,
Lift your arms bellowing joyous sighs;
Run after the dog as you laugh,
Use your magic baton like a walking staff;
Now spinning in circles until you fall
On the ground with arms out in a satisfied sprawl
Now rolling in the grass, your baton a-twirl,
Such a happy little giggling super girl.

By Morgan Cottrell

Poetry by Riley Davis

Blind

I wish you could see what I hear
The colors of sound I can sing
A soft meadow brook on a warm summer day
Like the song of a sunset fading away

If you could just see what I hear
Where darkness no longer means 'lost'
Where a young child's laugh is the light in his face
And a whisper of love makes the world a bright place

It's simple to see what I see
Just close your eyes and be free
Feel the wind on your face as it whispers around
And when you open your eyes
Don't shut out the sound
And just listen to what I can see

By Riley Davis

Distance

A look across the room
              our eyes meet
A connection so simple
              it startles

              A story is told there
                     your pains, your prides
                     your decisions, your life

                     It's only a moment we're looking
                            so fast
                     Can you see me so clearly
                            as I see you
                     Do you read in me the distance

a long ride, my life

I see what holds us back
          this connection
Now is not the time
          not our place
Pride, our fears unite us
          so simple

          A look across a room
                    The connection was made.

By Riley Davis

Time Watchers

It is a soft touch.
A slow engulfing of your senses.
A warm cloud of black that calms your mind and lets you rest.
Peace.

It is a slow ticking of the clock as you dream the fantastic.
Your imagination flies while your body unwinds.
The world settles down.
Peace.

Close your eyes.
Still your thoughts and just breathe.
A deep breath that cleanses your body and clears your heart.
Peace.

It is a quiet shout for a moment of your own.
Ten hours, five hours, three.
A soothing death.
Peace.

Stop a moment.
Rest.
Take a breath.
Peace.

By Riley Davis

Poetry by Thupten Tendhar

Help Me Create a New World

What if all the conflicts are resolved?
What if every yell is silenced?
What if entire families find reunion?
What if all broken hearts are soothed?

What if every missile is disarmed?
What if all the bombs are defused?
What if all enemies are reconciled?
What if every war is ended?

What if the guns are loaded with roses?
What if the cries transform into melody?
What if the tortures are stopped?
What if sad feelings are totally erased?

What if the stones of ego are ground down?
What if the arrow of humiliation is broken?
What if the hole of depression is patched?
What if the septic of stress is flushed out?

What if the suspicions are flattened?
What if the jealousy is melted?
What if the threats are quarantined?
What if the terrorism is wiped out?

What if the harsh words are eliminated?
What if the hatred mind is expelled?
What if the selfish attitude is eradicated?
What if the wrong views are corrected?

What if the hungers are fed?
What if the thirsts are quenched?
What if the shivers get warm clothes?
What if the poor are equally treated?

What if the animals are befriended?
What if the environment is protected?
What if the wildfires are prevented?
What if everybody shoulders responsibility?

What if the trees grow fresh green hair?
What if the sky sparkles its turquoise blue face?
What if stars twinkle their wonderful gold eyes?
What if the flowers blossom their vibrant brain?

What if the earth yields purely nontoxic foods?
What if the rivers flow clean potable water?
What if the oceans evaporate for timely rain?
What if the sun and moon shine without blockage?

What if the mountains stand without melting?
What if the ozone stretches out without wounds?
What if we renounce altering our ecology?
What if we realize harming others harms ourselves?

What if the children are taught peace?
What if the parents nurture absolute love?
What if teachers practice great compassion?
What if violence is rewarded none?

What if a big smile greets everybody?
What if strong arms embrace everyone?
What if bright cheers adorn each face?
What if a warm heart enriches every mind?

What if loving kindness becomes universal?
What if the people survive on infinite peace?
What if the Media finds no more dreadful stories?
What if we open a fresh whole new world?

What if every individual thinks for society?
What if the society takes care of individuals?
What if freedom exceeds cell phone coverage?
What if laughter roars louder than car engines?

What if the legislatures structure law for peace?
What if the executives run offices for harmony?
What if the judiciaries conduct hearings for justice?

What if serenity and prosperity glitter for all?

What if we cherish life more than materials?
What if we respect others more than ourselves?
What if we convert battlegrounds into Loveland?
What if we applaud peace more than violence?

Do I sound as typically childish as I am?
Do I look as awfully stupid as I am?
Do I gossip like an idealistic crazy man? I am.

But hey! What if you help make my dreams realistic?

By Thupten Tendhar
thuptendar@yahoo.com

Poetry by Richard V. Travisano

In Spain

Sunflowers as far as one can see,
(and you can see quite far)
all looking west at the setting sun.

And in the morning,
(with the sun tip-toeing up on the eastern horizon)
they all flip around
to greet the morning call to life itself.

Then all day salting away energy,
for the countless creatures of Spain
(from ants to aunts) to live their lives.

A sunflower sea,

with old castles atop every other hill island
(which impress time on one's mind).

Then a gay hot air balloon rising with the sun,
and I know the castles are solid stone illusions of the past,
and I have a date with a very present 747 in Madrid.

By Richard V. Travisano

Light

Being true to one's self, following one's heart — as it were,
may mean true love, or mere infatuation, or just going off on a sexual bender-
but whichever it is,
this getting to where you ought to be
lights you up,
your radiance balms the world, the whole world,
and as we say — all the word loves lovers.

So it's great! Beam! Shine! Light the dark (and some hearts as well).
No one "sensible" minds --

Unless (of course) it's with the "wrong" gender.

Now it's - "How?" "Why?" Whence this strangeness?
"Nurture!" some pundits say. (So, mom and dad did bad.)
"No, nature!" cry others. (Well, was it mom, or dad, who had the bad seed?)

Or did you choose to do, to be, this "what?" that no one but you (and other queers) want?

The morality dogs get their backs up, bark and snap,
herd you up with others, alike and akin, into your own circle.
Who are these fools who would disdain, cast out, some hues of the rainbow?
Repress, reject some lights the Gods choose to make this world shine,
which color flowers would they ban, which dark tree barks should be no more
which fruits are not to their tastes, which furry beasts, which spiders, wasps
or worms, dare to dance, fly and crawl outside the chocking boundaries of
their cramped dignity? Do even minerals offend? Is lead too heavy, mercury
too quick?

I say "Nay!'
to all censoring curtains, shades, wet blankets, and fire hoses;
all hues make light which brings –births--and nurtures life.

Yes! Embrace all light to see the Gods' creation and at last, get their message.

By Richard V. Travisano

Listen

Bright February morning
sun sparking off all-round snow
listen!
"Plink! Plunk! Plunk!
(maple sap dripping into buckets)
spring's earliest footsteps.

By Richard V. Travisano

Middlebridge Nights

Coming down Torrey Hill at night,
the Beavertail Lighthouse spashes
all over you every five seconds —

and at the bridge itself,
(if the sea is up and the air is moist)
you can hear the surf pounding the beach – (booming!)

and if you don't smoke, or don't smoke much,
you can even catch the fresh salt scent of the sea.

By Richard V. Travisano

On Re-meeting a Friend After a Decade [Does Lightning Strike Twice?]

I was looking forward
(I guessed)
to seeing you -

as I imagined
(or hoped)
(for your sake or mine?)
that you would be
sort of (you know)

like the way you are
(or seem to be)
instead of how you were
(not to mention how I was)
all those years ago.

But I told myself
"Stop dreaming!" because
she is not going to show
and (you know)
come by and say,
"Hi Richard!"
and take my hand
and (smiling)

whisper (mischievously)
"Damn everything but the circus!

By Richard V. Travisano

Pennies From Heaven

Stray pennies
    (tails is luck in Connecticut)
picked up
    (heads is luck in New York)
with impunity, and kept
    (in Rhode Island)
in an old sugar bowl.

Insuring (hopefully)
that he
    (cock-a-doodle-doo)
from Connecticut —
and she
    (cluck, cluck, cluck)
from New York ~
will remain long together
    (and happily too).

Of course this tack is silly, but why not —
especially when given,
that the official state bird is The Rhode Island Red Chicken!

(It's only pennies, Henny Penny, not the sky falling —

we hope.)

By Richard V. Travisano

Southern Spain Bus Trip: Huelva to Sevilla

Umbrella pines, fields of wheat, olive trees, castles on hills.
The Romans muscled in two thousand years ago,

the Moors somewhat later.

The Spanish waited them out,
and are here still –
 and are quite comfortable.

By Richard V. Travisano

Where Are The Mae Wests?

We've parted
        (so people are saying)
but we keep getting
        (separately or together)
into the same boat.

So I wonder
        (as I know you do)
whether we've parted
        (at all, after all)
and I worry
        (as you must too)
about these somebodyelses
        (wailing in the wings of your and my lives).

And we're holding each other so tightly,
and we're not at the wheel or the anchor,
and there's nobody else in the boat!

By Richard V. Travisano

Paintings By Maureen E. Cornell

Mansfield Hollow Dam

Unrequited

Short
. Stories .

Angela's Shame

Momma says young girls ain't supposed to sit by the river watchin' rats. What would the neighbors say? We're supposed to be at home learning how to cook and keep a home clean for our husbands. But I don't listen to her no more when it comes to that sort of stuff. Especially after what happened to Angela.

I was sittin' down by the river the other day watchin' for water rats and thinkin' 'bout what Angela had said. She said, "Ain't nobody gonna ruin it for me. No suh!" She was sittin' on the lawn chair in the back yard, smelling of Coppertone and sippin' a Tab with a straw. "Me and Ant'ny's gonna get married and have kids like a woman's supposed ta! I'm sixteen now and I'm not a little kid no more!"

Angela was pissed 'cause Poppa had laid down the law, sayin' she couldn't see Ant'ny no more 'cause she was only a teenager and had to finish school first and how he wasn't gonna let no kid from da hill knock up his kid. No Suh!

Well, first thing ya know, Ant'ny's throwing stones at her winda at night and she's whisperin' out the winda at him and then Poppa's out on the porch an runnin' 'cross the lawn and woulda got Ant'ny except he ran through the sand box and tripped over Armondo's Tonka truck and bucket. Shoulda see him though, flingin' dirt at Ant'ny, and Angela screaming and cussin' and momma standing in the doorway in her housedress and yelling' for Angela to close her winda or they was gonna send her to a convent.

Imagin' Angela in a convent? I mean, without a phone to talk on and having to cover her big hair and bangs? An' no boys? No suh! Not Angela. She'd run away first chance she got. Her friend Maria down at the beauty parla woulda helped her too.

I remember once, when they was still in junior high, she an Maria got caught peekin' in the cracked winda looking into the boys shower room in the gym. Poppa was furious and Momma kept crossing herself and sayin' this was God's way of punishin' her 'cause she didn't name Angela afta Poppa's mother.

It was at that time the boys began to notice Angela.

They started hangin' 'round outside the fence and rattlin' the chain link to make enough noise so Angela would look out the winda. And she would yell at them and call them all horny and to stop botherin' her but she would stay in the winda anyway and keep yellin' at them and twistin' her hair round her finga. Then Momma would come out to shoo them away and they would pretend like they didn't care if Momma was there or not, and as if it was their own idea to move on. As if they suddenly remembered they had other more important things to do.

And then Aunt Gilda started comin' over and talkin' to Angela about shame and God and what the baby Jesus would want her to do and how she oughta finish school because if she didn't we would all have to live in shame and if she let a boy do things to her, then the baby wouldn't be able to be baptized and wouldn't get into heaven when it died.

Well, Angela cried a lot at that and I think Aunt Gilda could see she was taking it serious and didn't want her baby to end up not in heaven.

So, she started goin' to church. Started going in the morning an' in the afternoons. Became crazed about it. Seemed to always be there and going to confession and then goin' to communion and then going back to mass again the next day. Momma started lookin' worried and started askin' Angela if she wasn't taking it a bit too serious and that maybe she was overdoin' it a little bit. But Angela didn't have none of it. She just kept goin' to church and prayin and confessin' an takin' communion. Poppa tried to keep her in once but Angela became sorta nuts and started hittin' him and yellin' and saying she had to go or her children wouldn't get into heaven and was out the door before he could figure out how to stop her without actually touchin' her body in a unnatural way.

Seemed Momma was ashamed to have Angela goin' to church all the time. But she was also ashamed if Angela was hangin' 'round with the boys. But you can't have it both ways. Either you live life or you don't. Momma and Poppa didn't get that. But then, we was Catholics and it seemed everything we did caused shame anyway.

That was one thing about being Italian and Catholic. Shame. And guilt. It seemed we was always under a cloud of shame and feeling guilty about it. Like we was always feeling ashamed and guilty that we was born because of a dirty sex act or somethin'.

Maybe that was why Angela started spending all her time at church. To clean herself of the dirty sex act.

Then one day we got a call from Father Griseldi. Angela was at the hospital. It seemed she left the confessional and was doing her acts of contrition and then fainted. Hit the floor and then started thrashin' 'round like some exotic dancer or somethin'. Her hands were bloody and at first Father Griseldi thought she had the stigmata and that a miracle was happenin' and he was gonna have to call the bishop. But then he realized that the blood was all over the front of her dress and runnin' down her thighs.

Seemed Angela had committed the dirty sex act and was pregnant but had lost the baby. Wasn't taking care of herself. Just prayin' and hopin' for a miracle. Well, her shame and guilt had done the job. The miracle had prevented her shame from showin' or bein' born.

Father Griseldi rode in the ambulance with Angela and blessed her and said a prayer for the baby. That seemed to help a bit. If the priest could pray for a baby that came from an unwed mother, then maybe, just maybe, the baby would go to heaven after all.

Angela didn't talk much after she came home. Just sat and stared at the floor.

Momma and Poppa was still ashamed of Angela though, and sent her to a convent anyway. They wasn't havin' their own daughter livin' under their roof and havin' all the neighbors knowin' that they had failed. If she was gone and livin' a holy life, then they could go on livin' in the neighborhood and pretendin' she was pure.

I guess that's another thing about being Catholic and Italian. Just because we pretend there ain't no guilt and shame, doesn't mean it ain't there just the same. No Suh!

By Richard Muto

Birthday Breakdown

When I pictured my nineteenth birthday, the image of being stranded at a cheap motel in Merrick, New York with no reservation, no car, and no idea how to get back home never came to mind. I hadn't planned for my scrappy little Cavalier to break down twice in one day – but that's what happened.

My boyfriend and I had envisioned the day much differently. He'd drive, of course, seeing as it was my birthday and I'm not the most skilled driver (which has absolutely nothing to do with being a woman – I'm just that I'm haphazard). The weather would be sweet and summery, with a sprinkle of clouds to ease the heat and the soft hum of singing insects in the background, far off in the woods and away from bothering me. If traffic was bad, so be it! We'd take turns plugging our IPods into his stereo and watch as Connecticut and New York passed by. The waves at Jones Beach would be enormous. I'd jump in first and he'd follow a little more cautiously behind, and when we were both worn-out and sick of the heat, we'd head over to the stadium across the street to watch the concert before going home.

That was how we hoped our first trip to Long Island would go, but this is what really happened. I pulled up to my boyfriend's house exhausted, because I stayed up ridiculously late watching amusing videos online the previous night (entirely my sister's fault – she's the one who sent me the initial youtube link that started the awful cycle). I had to finally tell myself to go to bed before the sun peeked up over my windowsill and caught me with my eyes open. The lack of sleep wasn't a big deal though – I could just doze off for a few hours in his car. Small, cramped napping spaces never bothered me. I grew up sleeping in a twin bed that took up half of my room.

The front door of his house creaked open and there stood a slouched, droopy-eyed version of my boyfriend. "You ready to go, Danny?" I asked with as much enthusiasm and spunk as I could muster up. "Let's go, I want to see the concert!"

A guilty smile crept across his face that made me feel a little uncomfortable. The first thought that came to my mind was that his dogs ate the concert tickets.

"So I know I said we'd take my car and all," he mumbled, "but do you think you could drive today? I'm really tired. I couldn't sleep for more than an hour last night."

Ok, so now it's a sleepy contest – who's the least able, functioning driver here? We decided to take my car because he had a better excuse for being tired and I actually like the taste of coffee. After a mandatory stop at Dunkin Donuts, we began our multiple-hour journey across the state and around to Long Island in my younger, less-experienced car. Never had a problem with the Cavalier so far, so why should I now?

Halfway into our hot, congested road trip, I noticed an unfamiliar glowing red icon on the dashboard of my car. It was my engine light, but neither I nor Danny were automobile experts, so we both shrugged off the warning light as a minor anomaly that would resolve itself on its own.

The highway was littered with stop-and-go traffic and even with the air-conditioner blasting at high power, the sun seeping through the car window made me feel like a not-so-Happy Meal sitting under a heat lamp. Danny didn't notice under his sleeping lids, but there was a bead of sweat dripping down his neck. I wanted to wake him up and tell him that the engine light was still red, but he looked so peaceful in his cool, restful state. I was just hoping that the car wouldn't explode in the meantime.

As we entered Hempstead, literally minutes away from our destination, the little ignorable warning light on my dashboard started to demand attention. All the lights were blinking zanily now and the volume on my radio was fluctuating in and out as if a poltergeist had taken over the controls of my car. This was it, I thought, karma getting back at me for forgetting my mother's birthday last year. On top of all the panic, chaos, and snoring from my boyfriend beside me, I happened to notice that my fuel gauge was leaning dangerously far over the red line. This problem I knew how to solve. I straightened up in my seat and carefully moved over into the right lane to get off the closest exit. With practically every light in my car blinking and the radio controlling itself, I rolled up next to a gas pump with the remaining drop of fuel I had left in my tank and turned off my car along with all the horrible warning lights. This was about the time when Danny woke up.

"Oh good, you getting some gas," he yawned. "Are we close?"

"Yeah, only about a mile or two, I think." I didn't want to tell him about the car. Maybe with a full tank of gas, everything would go back to normal.

Wrong.

The engine rattled the first few times I tried turning the key, but after that, barely even a hum. So there we were, seconds away from the beach and all the fun that had awaited us just to be stuck at a little gas station. This was breakdown number one.

I was stressed to say the least. The tow truck company was twenty minutes away, but said that they'd be at my car within the next two hours. Two hours? I couldn't stay here for that long in this ninety degree weather – I had to get my car running again, even if only for a few minutes. I was determined to get to Jones Beach.

With my hand on my hip and a firm foot on the ground, I convinced the two men working at the gas station to give my car a jumpstart. My boyfriend stood outside, next to my driver's window, watching and praying quietly for the men's truck to give my car life again. I kept my mouth shut as I heard the first three tries fail with the same death rattle noise as before. I was afraid that if I did open my mouth, I might cry.

Luckily, four was a charm that day. Relief drenched over my body like a cool bucket of water, causing strange laughter to bubble over my lips that even I didn't recognize. I thanked the men from the gas station several times, but I think driving away and out of their sight was more of a thanks than I could ever give.

The beach was just as beautiful as I had imagined. We played in the massive waves and fed the seagulls strange leftovers from our lunch – I had no idea a seagull could or would eat a peach pit.

The beach and the concert part was wonderful - went just as planned with no truly memorable moments - but then when it was all over and time to go home, the chaos started again. This time I knew we couldn't rely on another car for a jumpstart to get us back home, so we had to call a tow truck.

And now, we are back to the beginning of this story. The car was in the shop five miles down the road, waiting to be fixed in the morning, while Danny and I were sitting in the lobby of a tiny motel, hoping that the man behind the counter would be able to find us an open room. Due to some wonderful, miraculous turn of events, a woman called the motel that very moment and cancelled her reservation for the night. Once again, strange bursts of laughter spewed forth my mouth.

The room smelled of smoke and the television only offered three channels, but none of that mattered. Together, Danny and I cuddled in bed and leaned our two tired souls against one another.

"I'm so sorry that I had to put you through all this craziness," I said. "I wanted this all to be so perfect."

He kissed me on the head and pulled my hair back out of my face. "Honestly," he said, "I couldn't be happier that this all happened, because I get to spend a whole other day and night with you. So maybe the car breaking down situation was a little hectic at the time, but now that I look back on it, I realize that this day – my nineteenth birthday – would have never been as memorable if it wasn't for all the unpredictable parts. Life is crazy and hardly ever goes as planned, but if you take a few risks and keep a positive attitude, everything will work itself out in the end.

"Happy Birthday Babe!"

By Melissa Toni

Cliff Walker

It was late and we were tired. We rattled up the darkened road in a cramped old Chevy, packed inside like screws in an over full jar, but warmer for it. The higher we got, the thinner the cold, shadowed air became until the black clouds themselves were seeping through the cracks around the doors and joining us inside that beat-up car. With every twist in the road we were pushed closer together, elbow to elbow, ankle to ankle, four to a row and two to a seat. The turns started coming faster until we were snaking our way through dense rainforest and over jagged cliffs like some bizarre, half-blind beetle, continuing forward only for lack of a better option. Go. Go, for stopping was surely death; wild animals or other cars, bad people who would rape and kill us for sport. Fear; like a sour taste in the back of your throat, bitter, unpleasant, and unspoken. Slower and slower we went as roots made their way across our path, as boulders made their homes on the road and animals flashed passed our headlights like apparitions.

We were tired and it was late. Thoughts were becoming harder to hold onto. Breath was harder to grasp. The air was so thin that movement should not have been the heavy burden it was, but it weighed on us until we staggered out of the car like ancient men and women, centuries older than we should have been. Dark and humid, the open air pressed closer to us than the cramped cabin of the car. We spread out, putting distance between us, grateful for the space but with an itching on our backs; stumbling and weaving to find rocks to sit on or trees to rest against, needing the support of something solid to lean on.

One step, two. The crunching of the rocks was muted by the night. Indistinct shapes emerged from the darkness creating a cage of black hemming us in, herding us out. The car's headlights struggled to pierce the dark, but its poor wavering light extended no more than a few feet out in front. We were blind; creatures of the day, at the mercy of the night.

I struggled to a rock on the side of the road, gasping for breath. The altitude blurring my vision and clouding my head. The darkness shifted, looming up behind me, crawling over my shoulders and under my feet. I stepped back and the world dropped away, no flash of light, no startled scream, just blackness.

By Riley Davis

Creation Myth

In the beginning there was nothing; a large absence of existence, complete darkness. One thing that stood out in the distance, in all this darkness however was a little speckle of light, shimmering ball of life that twitched with motion. This ball of life was the only piece of existence in this nothingness and on one day something miraculous occurred. The ball of light exploded throughout the black umbra, shimmering, shining, flashing; and yet as quick as it dispersed it came back together. As it did something was created, a small baby child. That child was the essence of life and the beginning of existence, that child was the goddess of creation.

She was so small, so fragile, yet in the midst of two days she matured into a young adult, and with her maturation came knowledge, and consciousness. It was with this knowledge, this consciousness, and this sense of awareness that sprouted the goddess' first emotion: loneliness. She was in this dark world by herself, with no one else. The goddess cried and cried, her eyes pouring a deluge of salty tears. She was so sad, so lonely, all by herself and yet who would have thought something so depressing could be so productive. When the goddess finally sucked up her last sniffle and wiped the tears from her eyes she was amazed at the sight below her. A huge body of liquid Could it have been created by her? Dazed by the beauty of her creation the goddess grew with curiosity and reached out to touch this liquid, this thing she called the ocean. Amazingly, this shivering feeling of cold refreshment ran up her skin, leaving behind a trail of strange bumps. The goddess loved this incredible phenomenon and thus tried to fall from the darkness into the ocean, yet her efforts proved useless.

The goddess then thought to herself, "Wait, if I was capable of creating this ocean, what else am I capable of doing?" The goddess then took a deep breath and sighed releasing a tremendous gust of frustration wrought wind, and as she sighed, her body moved slightly closer to the ocean. It was then that the goddess formed an idea. Taking in a deep breath, filling her lungs with oxygen, she blew out a whistling wind from deep within and with its power she fell from the darkness. Splash! The water erupted about her as she fell bringing back that same familiar chill from before. The goddess arose from the ocean, chuckling and wiping the water from her porcelain face, clearing her eyes to bear witness to her newest creation...something she liked to call the sky. As happy as she was, the goddess swam and played in the ocean for quite some time.

It wasn't very soon however that the goddess grew tired and cold from the winds grace and the water's chill. Shivering she wrapped her arms tightly about herself, rubbing for warmth and trying her hardest to think of some way to escape the two elements for now. Rubbing at her skin, the goddess developed a new idea as her hands graced the very bumps that sparked her curiosity and thus she placed her arm before her. She then leaned over and bit a small piece of her skin off, to use for creation. The wound did not last long, however before it could completely heal a small drop of blood escaped into the water beneath and as it dispersed within it blossomed with life, sprouting all different types of creatures. There came turtles, fish, eels, crabs, and the complete life of the ocean. Surprised the goddess grew slightly distracted, but took a mental note and continued with her previous thought.

With both hands, the goddess compressed the tiny piece of skin from earlier and as she released and opened them up that same tiny piece expanded beyond belief creating what the goddess called the earth. It was the bottom of the ocean and at times rose up above, those old bumps becoming the hills and the mountains. The hairs about the skin shot up towards the sky and grew with life, spiraling and wrapping together to create the trees, plants and flowers. The goddess, now out of the water was so thankful, but still wet, and thus still very much cold. She huddled up, holding her body close to herself and did the first thing that came to mind. She remembered rubbing her skin earlier helped to keep her warm and thus began to rub her hands together vigorously.

 The goddess did not like this feeling, this shivering freeze and thus with much dedication the goddess rubbed and rubbed creating a warm friction in her hands. It was not long before a strange glow began to radiate from them, and so curiously the goddess opened them up to take a peek inside. What she saw was something she liked to called fire, sparking and dancing with heat, and oh it was very hot. Quickly trying to avoid the sting the goddess threw the ball of fire into a nearby bush and watched as it exploded into flame. What amazed her however was the fires capability to last as it ate up the bush and its life. She slowly moved closer, inch by inch, and as she did her skin grew warmer and warmer. She loved the sensation and so she grew close and took a seat nearby. Within seconds, the goddess was nice and toasty. However a feeling from before arose again, these creations were simply distractions. She was lonely once more.

The goddess then began to sob, tears pouring from her eyes once again. She watched as the tears grew close to the fire but could do nothing to stop them from coming, so she gathered her efforts to try and scoop the water back before it reached her flames. What came from this was a sticky messy muck, something the goddess called mud. Surprised, the tears stopped flowing and in its place came a feeling of curiosity so the goddess gathered up some mud and headed back to the ocean. Peering into the oceans mirror like surface, the goddess used her image as a reference and began to sculpt away at the mud, slowly creating something more complex then all of her other creations. In time, she molded together a mud doll in the image of herself. It was almost exactly like her, with arms and legs, eyes, a mouth, etc. She had someone else now, someone to talk to, and thus, excited she began to speak. Talking and talking the goddess tried her hardest to communicate with this doll however to her revelation, there was no reply. Frustrated the goddess threw the doll to the side and stared off into the sea with watery eyes.

She watched closely as the fish swam about, so graceful, so beautiful, and so full of life...and where did that life come from? The goddess thought to herself and quickly she came to a conclusion. She turned clumsily, almost falling onto her face and grasped the doll in one hand. With the other she placed her finger in her mouth and pierced her skin with her tooth. That same red liquid from before appeared on her finger, the life force within the goddess and with no time to think, and with no careful movement she dripped two drops of blood from her finger by mistake. One drop landing on the mud doll and one other on the balls of mud that dripped beneath it. Her eyes now began to twinkle with amazement as she watched a miraculous transformation unravel before her.

There in front of her appeared one being very much like herself as well as many smaller beings, of all different sizes and shapes. Some had feathers; others had fur, some with scales, and more and more. The goddess shrieked with happiness, scaring away all of the minor creatures into the caves, mountains, trees and the sea as she ran to this other being, this thing she called a human, hugging it and kissing it all over its beautiful face. She then took this human's hand and walked over to the fire to share with it stories and experiences. The goddess finally had a friend, and she was very thankful. Over time they shared everything and created everything, music, art, games and more. One thing she never noticed however was that her friend was growing older with each passing day.

Then there came one day, the day that the goddess learned one thing she wished she did not. This was the day that the human told the goddess that it felt like it could no longer live, the day the human told the goddess of its need for an eternal sleep, the day the goddess would learn of death. The goddess was so distraught, so disgusted that this human was so weak and vulnerable to the world around it. Why was this human not strong like her. However it was this morality that made the human so beautiful, this flaw about it was a key to its charm. Because of this the goddess was deeply saddened and scared for what was about to happen.

Not knowing how to deal with death, the goddess left her lover on the earth below, returning to the darkness forever. With everyday that passed the goddess watched from above as its human grew closer and closer to its end...and she could not bear to watch, she could not bear to see her lover die and once again she weaved an idea together. The goddess placed her hands about her chest and closed her eyes tightly as a soft light appeared within her palms. This light was similar to the light that created the goddess herself, the little fleck of shining light in the darkness. Taking this ball of light to her lips, she graced it with a kiss and sent it down to her lover. She was not ready to let her human go, and thus her plan came to life. The sphere of light traveled fast down past the sky and down to the earth.

The human could hear her voice now, and could see a bright light in the distance. It opened its eyes and with its last breath of life accepted the gift with open arms, and what happened next the goddess called a miracle. The sphere of light consumed the human and came together, compressing tightly, shaking with force, shaking with power. In two days the sphere shrunk and grew, and on the last hour of the last day the sphere exploded with light, with life. The goddess had given new life to her lover, splitting her human into many, many people, many colors, many shapes and many sizes and just as the goddess was capable of creating life, she had given them the gift to create life. Call it an act of selfishness, call it childish, but through this means, the goddess would never be separated from her lover. Through the cycle of life and death, creation and destruction the goddess could never be separated from her love, her human, or now, her humans, and thus she was happy. Even when loneliness crept too close to comfort, humanand goddess could still keep in touch and grow close, and this was through the act of love making, a ritual that kept both hearts beating as one.

By Matthew Silva

Dancing with Mount Washington

Let's get it out of the way straight off: I dance like a white guy. This is not to say I have no rhythm, as I have plenty. What I do is exercise a high degree of restraint while in the throes of exuberance. I insist though, that the rhythm is there for those of keen eye. Modesty with a groove; that's it.

This morning it's my exuberance that carries me to the dance floor well beyond the Greenleaf Hut, the rest of the party hav1ng faded into a bouquet of wallflowers. The music has taken over. Every step is on a whole note; each heart beat on the quarter. Every forth breathe swells to release that crescendo snort through the nose, while I carefully place my breathing at close to five thousand feet.

As with the best of music, I feel far more than I hear. I settle into a rhythm that caries me forward, and beyond. Then again, sustained winds of nearly 50 knots on the ridge approach made it nearly impossible to distinguish anything in particular from the din (save the syncopation of gusts surging at close to 70 knots). Any gust might well up evenly, and I could lean back into it as if to take some of the weight off my feet. Sweet legato. The next one might slam me across the back like being hit with a flying mattress. Bold staccato. Then I wobble the doe-see-doe with the trekking poles (I had the sense to back for the evening out) rising onto the balls of my feet while keeping the knees slightly bent. I am relaxed, and the rhythm moves me on.

This is a good thing, as what attention I can muster is drawn to the exploding canvas of the sky stumbling and whizzing low above my head. Surely the clouds' edges were ragged and frayed, were they to be seen at all. The other edge not on my mind was that of the rain harnessed close behind these frantic winds. According to the morning weather report issued from the

Mount Washington observatory, the rain too had laid claim to a number on today's dance card.

For now though, the rain jacket was worn to hold in a little heat. No hypothermia to spoil the mood, thank you. The jacket clung as though painted on the windward side. Downwind it puffed out like a spinnaker, even with zippers, drawstring and cuffs cinched down tight. I set the trekking poles wider than normal and well out front so they could lead as I follow. Rather than swinging the pole along with each step, I reach out and find purchase ahead of the step like the flam before the downbeat in a tight shuffle. This keeps me on my feet well enough until I gain the ridge and turn north. Now I crab a bit sideways on the knife edge to keep the southerly wind straight on my backpack, and avoid the sensation of having it grabbed and yanked only to leave me spinning clumsily from the torso down.

Dropping over the northern end of the Lincoln summit, I get into the lee and my gait relaxes accordingly. The Wagnerian drama in the sky above is strangely mirrored in the valleys below. The top of Owl's Head floats in a boiling cauldron of low clouds in the Pemi. Over my right shoulder I see a tongue of high clouds curl down over the backside of the Franconia Ridge. I glide readily and steadily forward. The footing is not at all greasy. I'm guessing it's about four more miles to the Garfield shelter, and I'm riding the groove.

It seems warmer here out of the wind so I stop and peel the jacket. A chug of water, and I saunter off, munching one of these organic, whole grain, high fiber, low guild granola bars. Following the cacophony of church, the ruckus of brawling air back there on the ridge begins to tail off like the clamor of the night club left half a block behind. Should I fumble for my keys? And can I remember where it was that I had parked? No matter. We're walking home and I've less than three miles now to go.

Partners change often enough to keep things fresh. Thin, soft, and pale green stretches move in close. I float gently along and relish the intimacy. Next in line waits a homely scramble. All tooth and bone, this one, with an awkward gait that has me thinking I'll be stepping on my own feet. The tempo changes as I climb higher up to meet her, but the rhythm stays strong enough for me to lead, and help my partner to look good. Of course, it *is* rather dark for noontime. Dropping over the back, the next in line waits with a quiet confidence that belies the course, gravelly exterior just now beginning to glimmer with the sparkling confetti of rain drops. And so continues the dance.

Now there is less than a mile to sanctuary and a chance to get off these aching feet. I imagine a fellow younger than I cranking ahead to his own feverish boogie beat, bashing through the precip like a giant clod in a crowded ballroom. In those years that was my style. Of course, it is not those years. Nor is it those miles. My style is the love child of all the years and miles I learned to stop counting some time ago. My style is evolving, and I'll be there soon enough.

So along I pace with that steady, subtle rhythm, felt more than heard; the rhythm of time's hammer on life's anvil. I feel a trickle of water creep out beneath my ear and run down the back of my neck, and someone whispers, *"If you dance, you will pay the fiddler."*

By John Lawrence

ESCAPE

A man chilled on an old rusted iron fire escape in Providence, Rhode Island, gazing into the streets two stories below him. The man's tattooed arms lead down to his hands one of which was holding a pen. A pad of paper was resting on his lap. A joint was in his other hand. He lifted it to his lips and leisurely puffed. The man held the smoke in for a long while and then let it out with ease. As he did, the smoke encircled the air and slowly disappeared as it floated up above and out of sight. A jacket barely cushioned the man and his pad as he sat on the iron slats of his fire escape writing and puffing—a half dozen scribbled pages, lettering squished in and printed sideways , some of which read:

> Words *are a window to the soul of their creator that when recorded and written down can be beautiful but if left alone and unwritten that beauty becomes fleeting in the seconds it takes to forget them, even by those who are the creator. In the world of words, silence and barren pages are.*

On the fire escape across the way might have been a mirror image at one time or another; but if that was true it wasn't any longer. A person sat on a beat up fire escape on the third floor. Her peach and hot pink color clothes were slightly grimy, in tatters, and she also held a pen; though, it was hollowed out and held between her lips. The pen was connected to an old, beat up soda bottle as she wrote in her mind with the smoke that trailed out from her nose, and her mouth, and her homemade pipe. Her thoughts disappeared as quickly and quietly as the smoke which encircled her head; and, like the man across the way, the smoke too disappeared as it floated in the same direction. Perhaps the wind also carried her invisible words up above and out of sight.

A short distance below in his squad car was a police officer. He observed; but, for whatever reason, at the time, he did not particularly care. He was a beat cop with not much drive on this night—as stark and rigid as they come.

A few groups of teens swaggered down the street, one group on one side and the other headed in the opposite direction on the opposite side. They were wild and rowdy and unaware of the people on the fire escapes as they passed underneath them. They merely continued on with all of their rowdiness about them and paid no mind to their surroundings—police included.

Beyond the fire escapes in both directions there were similar houses lined up and down the block with an occasional car that passed by; the street ran straight and the cross roads could be seen for a few blocks on; but, then, was tapered out of view for the street became curved right where the abandoned factories began. Along the way, as in all inner cities, there was a never ending row of telephone poles that stretched along with the street, every now and again one would jut out with some anomaly from a car hitting it or perhaps just because it was created that way. The sound of traffic, gunshots, and music could be heard in the not so far off distance.

Around one of the corners, down an otherwise unnoticeable alleyway, was a group of overly talented graffiti artists—spraying away their cares onto the grimy canvas alleyway walls and junky artifacts that were strewn about. Spray cans were on the ground, the caps off and carelessly thrown to the ground, and the fingers of the artists were stained with paint. A man stood peering around the corner, on the lookout for cops, his right hand resting on his piece. He did not move. The two people on the fire escapes remained. The man kept still and barely moved but for his pen. The girl on the fire escape stared into the open air like a gargoyle overlooking it all but seeing nothing. The cop still sat and stared into his computer and then glanced around. He was holding a cell phone to his ear but didn't seem to be speaking at that moment.

The man who wrote was nearing or just surpassing his 30s. He grew up in the city but was determined not to make it all he knew. His name was Dimiour Gikos but he was known as D'jour around the city. He was tattooed, and when he wasn't sitting, he was tall and walked briskly. Underneath his Yankees hat his hair reached out from the roots and down in braids so sharp that it seemed as if they would never become frazzled or frizzed out. D'jour's face was not oval, it was more elongated yet proportionately correct with beautiful hazel eyes. He was clean-shaven at the moment but was known to wear a goatee or sometimes a line beard. He was a writer of stories who depended on his surroundings and experiences to write. After all, one can only write about what he knows or what he can imagine; yet, what he imagines is based on what he knows.

Across the way, the lady began to stir; she was no longer still. Her name was Eley Theria. Once, people simply called her Ellie; but anyone that knew her was long faded from her life by now. Possibly the only people who knew her name now was D'jour and the postman. He had received junk mail for the building across the street on a semi-regular basis—mostly writer renewal notices and furniture advertisements.

Ellie had finished her score and was annoyed that there was no more of what she both loved and despised. She reached in her pocket and found an empty candy wrapper, which she gently pushed off the fire escape and then she cried lowly and mutably. She drew away a brown paper towel that was partially under her leg, which she had been sitting on. With it, she wiped her face and nose, opened the paper towel up again and tossed that off as well. She watched it float down.

Ellie swiveled on her slightly soiled peach colored pants and attempted to get up. She made it half way and then sat back down facing the opposite direction. Her stirring had alerted D'jour for all but an instant and then he flipped the paper and begun another page of writing. He imagined her life and things that she had been through to get to this low point. He pictured that there was some hope and some steps in her life that she would take to pull herself up.

As he wrote Ellie reached up, grabbed onto her rusty fire escape, and pulled herself towards the railing—she leaned over the side and looked down at the people swaggering over the cracks and lines in the pavement below. Her arms, which leaned upon the rail of the fire escape, seemed lanky and long almost as if they could reach out for a star and actually grab one. The rusty fire escape was the only thing holding Ellie out in mid-air among the stars; it squeaked with age as the woman leaned—the bottom of her forearms now stained with rust. Her face was old yet she was young. She looked at the smoke trailing off in the distance dissipating into the sky. A bat flying past caught her eye and it too had grown smaller and appeared to dissipate into the night. Ellie then looked out and up at the stars and imagined things that she never wrote down and are now of no consequence. The bat that seemed to have dissipated did not come back, but Ellie shifted her gaze and looked for it in the spot where she last saw it. The streetlights remained on though, and she slowly altered her line of sight and affixed her gaze on those instead. They seemed to give off streams of light in a downward direction, which ultimately pooled at the base of the pole for lack of room to cast any further.

He heard the sound of creaking metal and gazed over at the woman because, although it echoed slightly off the surrounding buildings, it certainly came from Ellie's direction. She seemed oblivious to the noise—or just didn't care. She gazed on and D'jour wrote it off as he wrote on. After a few moments he heard it again. This time it was louder and as he looked over at the woman, from her body language, she seemed to have heard it too. She stirred slightly and went back to leaning and staring into the city night. A third time his ear caught the creak of the metal and he realized it had to have been from the fire escape across the way.

D'jour then thought about her life and he wrote some more. The light from the city reached up and dulled the star's shine. That was the problem with the city it was harder to see the stars. But they were still there—the stars. And he still wrote.

"What if the metal gives way and she were to fall?" He thought as he wrote and he heard the sound again. Then he dismissed the idea as being ludicrous but thought twice. "It would be wonderful story for writing. Would she be able to hold on to the metal as it slowly bent and eased its way down to the point where he could rush to grab her? Could he make it to her on time? Would he even have to? She could make that." He imagined the sound that was being made could lead him to write a great story; and so he wrote:

"Suddenly, the sound of the metal made a horrible grinding noise and bent away from the house as if it had the intent on letting her down as gently as possible. Ellie held on tight and screamed—she knew that the rusty iron welding had given way and thought she would die. Her arms felt as though they had stretched enough to reach those stars she had stared at for so long. The stinging pain that she felt from the rusted metal on the palms of her hands was poignant and shot through to her lanky arms reaching her shoulders. As Ellie screamed the creaking metal platform bent with a sort of stiff ease down far enough to the street where she could let go. It seemed to her like it was happening in slow motion.

"Ellie's homemade pipe had fallen with her and out of the folds in her shirt a crumpled up cigarette cellophane with her drugs. She thought she had smoked the last of it but was too high to realize otherwise. Ellie was happy for a moment until she heard the piercing sound of the squad car roll up beside her. Her fear drove her to scramble and run grabbing the cellophane but leaving the pipe. The pipe could be made again from remnants held within garbage cans. As she ran one shoe fell off and she pounded the city pavement with one bare heel and a dull pain that was virtually unnoticeable crept up Ellie's leg like an inchworm on a leaf. She was barely conscious of it as she ran on a slight downgrade and with a sharp left through the freshly spray painted yet still filth ally. She had no thought penetrate her mind except to just keep running. She needed to get away from everything—the sounds, the smells, the city itself—just run. Ellie dodged her way through alleys and side streets, backyards and business lots.

"For an instant, she was unaware of how fast she was and that she had eluded the police officer. She hopped a fence and caught her arm on the sharpness of the chain-link fence. Ellie held up her hand and blood flowed in a steady stream down to her elbow. She examined the wound, made a feeble attempt to pinch it closed, and gave up deciding instead to walk on to nowhere in particular.

"As the night climbed on in hours towards the turning point of the day, Ellie's bloody arm dried and she was now in the city park. The trees grew thicker before her eyes and they waved as if cheering her on for a battle well fought. She picked at the dried blood and peeled it away bit by bit as if it were a skin to be shed. She took her fingers, pinched the scratch, and endured the discomfort so more blood could drip out--and she had blown on it to dry and peel away again. Her arm throbbed but it did not hurt as much as her heart pounded, and it was something for her to do. She was positioned limply on a tree-enclosed embankment breathing heavy still from that night's event. Ellie's body was telling her to stay—so for the moment she did.

"She led the flow of the freshly forming blood droplets with her fingernail down her arm in the opposite direction. As it dripped she blew on it some more. She suddenly felt eyes converging on her; it was some type of night animal and was more afraid of her. Stil, her heart beat faster and Ellie took a huge gasp of air into her chest. She felt as though the high was gone and now it was only her with her normal yet somehow dulled out awareness. She was nowhere near as sharp as she should have been but she felt otherwise. Some power in her being drove her to get up and move on away from that creature and that embankment. She saw its eyes and it was almost as if she could tell what the animal was thinking—but she really couldn't. Ellie felt a breeze upon her back as she walked away and swore she heard the animal's footsteps patter off in the other direction.

"She looked at the tree line in front of her and could see car lights breaking through; the highway was on the other side. She could see the trees waving in front of the all these headlights and could almost make out the shape of each individual branch. They were holding the cars on the highway. That was their purpose tonight—to cheer her on, protect her from view, and hold the cars on the highway. Ellie turned to the left and viewed lights flickering off and on. She decided to sit and watch for a while. It was as if she were watching a dance. The shades of shadows flickered back and forth and she could make out lightening bugs dancing along to the beat of the shadows. She closed her eyes and remembered the view from the fire escape. It could not even come close in awe to Roger Williams Park at night.

"She got up and walked semi-cautiously as she kept switching her view from the tree-lined highway to where she was headed in front of her. There, further on, stood the 'Temple to Music,' small in the distance and silent and serene in the moon-soaked darkness. As she walked closer to the 'Temple to Music' it grew larger with every step, and Ellie noticed columns simultaneously poked out and rose up from the night air. In the calm lake behind the temple ripples softly rolled at an angle. The lightening bugs speckled the tree-lined horizon and that line of trees behind the lake was soaking in the dull glow from the city lights. Ellie thought of the beauty of the world she was missing and longed for change."

Unexpectedly D'jour, still on the fire escape, heard something within earshot that pulled him up and out of his writings. It was a horrible metal creaking—magnified tenfold from the last creak. As he looked around and across to the other fire escape he noticed it was pulling away from the building. It was far away but closer in that instant as to allow him to hone his sight to the panic on Ellie's face and the worry in her eyes. The bolts had pulled out of the wall. Her face was riddled with lines that were now deeper than he ever noticed they were; and all that she had worried about in the past was nothing compared to this moment.

The first jolt of the fire escape had caused Ellie to be paralyzed with fear; the next caused her to lose her footing and tumble over holding on to the rusted metal with her grime encrusted fingertips. Her "Help me!" scream echoed off of the buildings and down the street catching the ear of the graffiti artists. To them her call was like a sick cat crying at the top of its lungs. The sound reverberated down the alley and through their ears with a sharpness the penetrated their deepest being, giving chill-bumps to the even the bravest one in their team.

Although he was no expert, D'jour knew the outcome of the situation if Ellie were to fall. Within seconds, the police officer called in the emergency and was under the woman calmly shouting to her to hold on. The officer tried the front door but it was locked. He called up again for the woman not to let go and say help was on the way.

D'jour noticed Ellie held on tight—as tight as she could, as split seconds mounted into seconds and a crowd gathered around her. The clanging of the ladder of the fire escape echoed in the ears of all who were near, in awe, and gasping, the escape ladder was being pulled down to the ground by the spray-painters from the alley. One had sat on the others shoulders to reach it. D'jour heard that sound and thought Ellie must feel the vibrations in her palms, fingers, and fingertips. Fingerprints of red and yellow stained the rusted, bottom rung where the ladder was grabbed to pull down. The officer pushed everyone back and refused to let them on the ladder citing it was far too dangerous and called again for backup in a slightly more panicked tone. Some of them protested but most listened for the moment.

As D'jour rushed in his window, through his apartment, and down the dark light-lacking stairwell he felt his heart pounding and lungs pulsating.

In the same moments D'jour was hammering down the stairs, he imagined a million thoughts about Ellie. How she felt her palms give way to just her fingers and tips; she was slowly slipping. She wrenched her head this way and that and saw all the people gathering below her. He thought she wondered why she heard sirens but didn't see any flashing lights coming from either direction because in her mind she had been there forever. Thoughts were racing through his mind about her thoughts and actions. How her legs stopped flailing almost the moment she flipped over and just seemed to have hung like dead weight. How she would change her life after this ordeal.

Meanwhile, the spray-painting crew was at it again; they were attempting to climb the fire escape ladder to rescue her. The officer pulled out his tazer on the growing rowdy crowd and demanded they step back.

D'jour felt himself winded and crushed as people pointed. The buildings, the fire escape, the people, they were all distorted, like looking at a Monet that is touching one's nose—This was what he saw as his head, heart, and lungs all pounded in rhythm. It was as if he, himself, were in one of those paintings looking into another. He made his way through the crowd that grew to an enormous density in just a few short moments. There were double the police officers there now and they noticed him barreling through the crowd; they attempted to head him off. He dodged them as the crowd shifted. He swiveled around to the spray-painting crew and attempted to assist them in another rescue attempt. They were half way up the escape when suddenly, D'jour snapped out of his thoughts as he emerged from his front door and looked up.

Ellie was no longer there. She was in mid-fall. She had struck an air conditioning unit before hitting the ground with a thud. He was no longer with his thoughts in his mind full of wonder. He was thoughtless, motionless, wordless, and breathless all at once. And as D'jour stood there a single tear rolled down each cheek. He saw her body twisted and broken lying lifelessly in a pool of blood just a few feet in front of him. All his fanciful writings could not change the fact that Eley Theria was now dead.

By Carrie Anne Perez

Evade Responsibility

The last euro dropped into the machine with a clang of finality. Glancing back at the directions, I pushed in a four-digit pass code and pressed enter. Nothing happened.

I stood and stared dumbly at the machine which had just eaten an entire euro of my carefully-counted and systematically-horded money. I grabbed the locker I had chosen in a grip of death. I pulled and heaved, jangled and rocked, I even kicked it a few times, but it wasn't going to open. I needed this locker; Glori and I couldn't leave our packs in the tent and we certainly couldn't carry them up and down the mountain on our way to the city. My fist slammed the locker as I pushed myself away.

"Ello."

I must have jumped a foot straight up in the air, too busy brooding to pay attention to people sneaking up on me. Whirling, I assessed the man now standing in front of me and found a kid, maybe a year or two older than myself, sporting a huge grin completely unbefitting of the situation I was currently in.

"It din'a work for me either. You 'ave ta put in the numba first, then th' money. The poster lies." He chuckled at me.

Doubtful, I turned back to the poster to assess the directions. "Mettere Euro. Entrare il numero di armadietto." Obviously, 'cause I speak Italian, Keith showed me what to do, chatting away in good-old English about his Venezuelan dancing wife and life as a traveling puppeteer. We finally got the blasted locker working and bundled up on Keith's warning that the temperature would drop at night. We slept tight our first night in Florence, Italy.

I woke to the sound of my own teeth chattering so hard I thought my brain would rattle out of my head. It was cold! I struggled out of the sleeping bag-and-blanket pile that my bed had become, dragging my clothes out with me. I changed with lightening speed while they were still warm from being in the bag with me all night. Peering over the edge of the bunk bed I saw the shivering mound of cloth that was my Latina friend.

Grinning evilly I poked her. "Wake up, Sleeping Beauty. You should probably get dressed while it's still warm out." I dodged the sock that came hurtling at my face and stood back to enjoy the stream of tri-lingual curses that flowed from the shivering pile. I chuckled, somewhat envious of the ease in which Glori could express the situation. The best I could do was "bloody cold!"

We have to ask ourselves, "Why did we choose to sleep in a tent on top of a mountain in Italy in the middle of February?" The answer, plain and simple, was we were broke. The night before we spent sleeping in a bus stop in Siena because we had miscounted the number of nights to book at the hostel and couldn't afford another one. Now we were freezing our butts off on a breathtaking mountain top and enjoying the hell out of ourselves. Well I was, and Glori would, once she thawed out.

By Riley Davis

Familiar Ambiguity

I met Ambiguity on a stretch of road where you might not expect to see another soul. Ambiguity smiled with an expression that cast its position like a net into deep implications. Ambiguity began to talk me up about family, and quickly reminisced on the photo that his Mom took proving that Vagueness and him were kissing cousins. Her father Paradox found a variety of uncertainty that led to meeting his wife Perception, but it seemed that life for Vagueness would never remain stable for any length of time. Perception it seems had moods that could flip flop at any unexpected turn. This he confessed made Vagueness fear that she was somewhat dwelling in discontent because at any moment life could just be unclear. "The Ambiguous family pedigree is distinctly comprehensive," Ambiguity said. He spoke with a shy expressiveness as he told of being from here and there, in an accent I couldn't really place.

As we walked together it seemed it could have been hours that passed in the short time we chatted. Somehow I felt I was nearing my destination even though it was nowhere in sight. The thought of home brought to mind those we love. When Ambiguity spoke of his love, Inconsistency, it seemed that he glowed. She was pregnant with twins but they both believed that they were going to be unable to name their children. When asked, Ambiguity's Uncle Paradox said "Quasi, Pseudo, and Exception" with a sly grin.

"I thought you said your wife was having twins?" I asked a little confused. Paradox smiled too and paused as he looked at me.

"It seems when I asked Paradox he was divided by self contradiction."

"So what did you do?"

"Unsure of how to proceed I asked him again and he said, 'Entendre is having twins and you're going to be the proud parent of two beautiful boys'.".

"Entendre isn't who you asked about", I said.

"I know and I was scared to ask another question. So I am off to Innuendo's house. He's had this kind of thing happen before." Ambiguity said ,rushing away. I had a feeling though, that the pun wouldn't stop there. Smile.

By Joseph A. Santiago

Frustration

One "should," stacked too close to another, recently leaned a little too much on my positive outlook. The day can stack those shoulds so they lean if I take the wrong perspective with me. When that happens, I can should on myself without hardly thinking on it. Frustration peeks behind the corner with sleepy eyes and yawns. Peeking is like peeping when the moment is right. Everyone is ready to jump on as they are busily bumping into their coulds. When I could take a nap, I am tempted to take her to bed and pull up the covers to tuck us in. Yet the delight of a job well done, and at times getting it done once and for all, frustrates me from sleep.

How is it that my mind can buzz away through dreams? I used to think it was my snoring, but now I know it is my ideas grinding loudly so that I wake up planning from dreams. Dreams are tricky stages of performance art, all put on to play with our own musings. Always made from scratch and better with practice, my dreams will sometimes taunt my frustration before the favor can be returned. My dreams deliver a magic wand and frustration will produce a magic marker ready to move the obstacles in an impish duel. Both sides creating and steering attention with their strengths to challenge the spirit and pull along my daily mind even when it says "quit".

Such illogical logic wills my emotion be sweetened to rouse me from my bed. My plans are the squeezed nectars of frustration's wild vines. So quickly can this vine become a weed that I have needed to remember to sip and not devour the indulgent berry or else my stomach may turn. While it may be nice scenery seeking to take two lefts to make a right, frustration's fruit keeps my attention on this one way to view to see. Once this mental buzzing takes my attention to somewhere else to dream and be, frustration must follow with flower and form in hopes to attract me.

When moving ideas from here to there it is very hard to stop and stare. Take it all in because frustration will wait, and it is the views of perspective that move my gaze from the flowery shadows of my daze. Nothing pricks and pinches me more than forgetting about the stunning tickle of getting lost in a thicket of frustration.

By Joseph A. Santiago

Injection

Sweat broke out over his skin and his eyes shifted restlessly. Faces were staring at him; angry, hateful faces. They had wanted him dead for what he did. They had hunted him through the filthy allies like a pack of starved dogs where fear had been a physical thing, choking the breath from his lungs until red bled down his vision and the air around him became wool.

Cold like glass shot shards down his chest to his arms and up the base of his neck. He thought of struggling but the thought was never manifested in his movements. Black fog was clouding his vision around the edges and creeping up his legs in stark contrast to his arms.

Twenty years ago he had thought this was a fitting punishment for the crime; obliteration, nothingness. Forgiveness is not needed when the very footprints of a soul are erased from the memory of the earth.

A sigh pressed past his lips. His eyes slid closed, blocking out the truth. A waiting calm was bubbling inside him and he wondered vaguely if this was one of the effects. His fingers slipped from the grip they had held on the plank of wood he had used to steady himself. Panic lurched through him then swept past as if it had been just a gust of wind.

As the last shreds of who he was combated the emptiness growing inside him he cracked an eye open for one last look at the world that was about to forget him.

By Riley Davis

The Ladies

Iona tapped her long red fingernails against the steering wheel and heaved out a long sigh into the warm oppressive Louisiana night.

"Well, girlfriend, now what do we do?" asked Fulla in the back seat, giving her best Pearl Bailey facial expression.

Deb, sitting next to Iona in the front seat, leaned over and put her hand on Iona's shoulder. "What's the matter? Why have we stopped?"

"It's the radiator and thermostat. I need new ones. Sometimes it gets too hot and the car shuts down for twenty minutes till it cools off again," Iona sighed.

Deb checked her wristwatch and reached over to the dashboard. "Can we listen to the radio at least?"

"Oh sure, just run the battery down, too, while you're at it," lamented Fulla, snapping open her small red fan, which matched her red satin and feather dress, and quickly batted air against her face.

"Well, it's better than listening to you bitch all night long," shot Deb over the front seat. Her silver lame` dress was tight and hot and she was getting irritable.

"Seems to me, listening to me is the only thing you're going to be doing with anybody tonight," retorted Fulla again.

"Pig."

"Whore."

"Bitch."

"Hag."

"Ladies, please!" Iona yelled over the loud voices in the confined space. "Can we just wait the twenty minutes in peace till the car starts up again and we can be on our way?"

Fulla leaned in to Natalie, her seatmate in the back. "What you smiling at? Think you never heard two drag queens going at it before."

"Female illusionists, if you please," Iona cut in scanning the back seat through the rear view mirror.

"Ouch," Deb complained. "The tape on my boobs is pulling too tight."

"Well you got nobody to blame but yourself," Fulla shot back. "Using half a roll of duct tape just to give yourself a bigger cleavage than me."

"Girls." Iona lamented.

"Wha-, why girl, look at you," Fulla scolded, pulling away from Natalie. You didn't even shave. What's wrong with you? At this rate we'll only have time to pull into the parking lot and run on stage as the curtain goes up and you got a five o'clock shadow. How about your legs, did you at least do your legs?" Fulla reached over and began pulling up the hem of Natalie's simple black dress.

"Leave me alone," Natalie pouted, pulling the hem of her skirt out of Fulla's reach. "I'm still not comfortable with this. You've been doing drag shows for a number of years now and this is only my second one. I'm a little nervous."

"And you should be nervous too," Fulla remarked looking out her side window. "I saw your first show. Looked like a bagman in a housedress. Mmm, mmm. Pitiful. I thought to myself, 'what's this world coming to?'"

"There's nothing to be nervous about." Deb said, reaching a comforting hand across to the back seat.

"Well you all have it easy," Natalie continued. "I've only been out for a few years. It's not like I came out when I was a teenager, like they do nowadays. I'm in my fifties."

"Girlfriend, ain't none of us had it easy, "Fulla replied, "Try being black, gay, fifty-two, and a drag queen."
Natalie's nerves got the best of her and she began to cry softly.

"Oh, look. Now you made her cry." Deb said, reaching out to rub Natalie's knee.

"Well, look. Since we have time, Natalie, why don't we two hop out behind to the trunk and fix you up a bit? I have an electric cordless razor in my make-up kit. Maybe we can even try a little blush and a foundation to highlight the contours of your pretty face." Iona offered, pulling the door handle, which illuminated the car's interior and her gold and black beaded **Bob Mackie rip-off.**

"Gonna need a trowel to apply that make-up," retorted Fulla.

"Fulla!" Deb said sternly, her eyes glaring icy darts at her.

Behind the car Natalie stood in an awkward stance while Iona inserted the key in the trunk lock.

"You got a cigarette"? Natalie asked.

While rummaging through the trunk, Iona reached under her wig and pulled a smoke out from behind her ear. "I thought you gave those things up," Iona commented.

"I thought so too." Natalie said, patting her hips, looking for a match that wasn't there. "I guess I'm just a little nervous. **You know, doing drag. Finally** admitting to myself that I'm gay. You know. All that stuff."

Iona continued rummaging through the trunk. "So, you came out recently, did you?" she asked.

"Yes," Natalie answered, "Three years ago. For the Bicentennial."

"I dressed as the Statue of Liberty for the Bicentennial." Iona said. Speaking over her shoulder, Iona asked, "Why'd you decide to impersonate women?"

"Well, you know. Growing up that's what we were told homosexuals did. They'd dress up like girls and do disgusting things," Natalie paused. "It's not like we had any role models around back then. At least we didn't realize it. I mean, there were rumors about certain teachers and there was some talk about the librarian, but, well, you know. It wasn't something people talked about in my day."

Iona just stood and listened. She figured Natalie needed to talk and just needed somebody to listen.

Natalie continued. "The kids at school pegged me for a fag right from the word go. I was beaten up every day at school from the third grade through high school. And then my father would beat me up for not being a man and standing up to them. Even the girls. They'd run up behind me and knock my books out of my arms and the other kids would start kicking them up and down the halls while we passed from one class to the other. But what really bothered me was the teachers. They just stood there and watched, as if it was okay for the kids to beat up on me because I was the class fag. And by the time I would collect my books from up and down the corridor, the late bell would ring and the teachers would berate me in front of the whole class for being late."

Iona waited till she was sure Natalie was finished. Then she turned back towards the trunk and opened her toolbox/make-up kit.

"Well, I think you're brave," said Iona pulling out the razor and blowing at its head. "Straight people don't understand. They thought we were the weakest kids in school but I'd like to see some of them survive what we were put through and live to tell about it. I bet I don't know of one single gay guy who didn't suffer complete humiliation in gym class every day."

Natalie gave a weak moist smile. "Yeah. What's so important about climbing some old harsh rope anyway? I'd like to see them do it today at our age."

"I'd like to see them do it in heels." Iona said.

"I like the fact that you use a big red metal tool box to hold your make-up," Natalie remarked, her eyebrows lifting upward as she peered over Iona's shoulder.

"It's the butch side of me. Actually, I think it sort of kicks the wind out of butch men's attitudes if I use it for makeup. I also have one at home for my sewing supplies."

What's the hot melt glue gun for?" Natalie asked.

"Honey, looking this pretty sometimes takes power tools." Iona responded. Natalie squinted her eyes into the dim trunk. "You also seem to have a lot of superglue. What is that for?"

"Darling, you'd be amazed at what keeps our fannies in these slim and confining sheaths of glamour. Superglue, hot melt glue, rivets, nuts and bolts, anything is better than having a safety pin let loose into your ass when you do a kick line." Iona laughed.

After Natalie was deemed presentable, Iona said, "Well, you're not one of Bette Midler's Harlots, but I think you'll do."

"As long as I don't look like Lillian Carter."

"Our president's mother would be thankful as well." Iona quipped.
They slid back into the car as headlights illuminated them from behind.

"Car's coming." Iona stated the obvious.

"Should I get out and wave a hanky for help?" Deb asked.

"No, I think you should wait right there. It's the police." Iona said looking through her rear view mirror.

A lone police office stepped out of his vehicle and slowly sauntered over to the driver's side of the car

Iona rolled down her window. "Good evening office. May I help you?" she asked.

"Good evening ladies. Having some car problems?"

"Yes officer, but we're all right. It just does this sometimes. Another five minutes and we'll be on our way again."

"Looks like you ladies are all dressed up. Going to a party or something?" the office inquired.

"Not really. We're entertainers on our way to a show." Iona said, giving her best seductive smile.

"Really? Are you strippers?" the cop asked shining his flashlight into the eyes of the ladies.

Iona straightened herself up in her seat while the other occupants in the car adjusted themselves and heaved disgusted sighs.

"No, officer. We're singers and dancers. We do fundraisers to raise money for local charities."

"Make more money being strippers," the cop said. "Sex and alcohol always makes money, no matter what the economy." He shifted his gaze towards Iona's cleavage, "You want to make money, ya gotta show a little something."

At this point the officer scanned his flashlight over the other ladies faces, focusing on Natalie who had shrunk down in her seat and kept her eyes downcast.

"Uh, maybe we should try to turn the engine over again, Iona, see if it runs now," Fulla said trying to divert the officer's attention away from their weakest link. Iona obeyed but the car still refused to budge.

"Actually, I suppose I should ask you for some identification. I mean, a carload of fancy dressed women struck out on a lonely country road. How about letting me see your driver's license?"

"You want to see my license?" Iona blinked. "But officer, we're totally fine. My car just shuts down sometimes when it overheats and it needs to rest for a few minutes. It's not like we were speeding or anything."

"Weren't even crawling," Fulla muttered under her breath.

"Well, that's fine ma'am but I still need to see your identification."

"He wants to see my license, ladies," Iona said not taking her eyes away from the officer's eyes.

"But we didn't do nothing," Fulla objected.

"Who asked you?! License! Now!" the officer barked.

Iona riffled through her purse and pulled out her identification. She handed it over to the policeman.

The office looked at it for a moment and his face screwed up in confusion. Then his eyes became stern and he shined the light back on to Iona. His light shifted down to her throat to reveal her Adam's apple, and then back up to her face.

"Holy shit! You're a fuckin' fag!" He yelled.

"Actually, we're female illusionists. I'm Iona Trailer, this is my friend Deb Utaunt," Deb waved her fingers and smiled, "and in the back is Fulla Valium and our newest friend is Natalie Dressed. As I said, we're perf-"

"I got me a car full of fags," the officer continued. "Out! Everybody out!" he ordered.

"But officer, we-"

"GET THE FUCK OUT OF THE CAR! NOW!"

"Such language," Deb tutted as she opened her car door.

The ladies stood in a line, Natalie trying to disappear between Deb and Fulla.

"Fags! I should 'a known."

"Actually, officer, not all drag queens are gay. Some are straight and have wives and kids an-"

"DID I ASK YOU, BOY?" the cop bellowed pushing his face up against Fulla's face.

Natalie whimpered.

"Well, well. What have we here? Scared fag? **Scared of what the big police** officer is gonna do to you?"

"Look officer, this really isn't necessary. We'll just start our car and be off to the show and there won't be any harm done," Iona offered hopefully.

"Off to a show. Gonna sing and dance for your fag friends?"

"Just dance, actually. We lip-sync to the music," Deb volunteered.

"You're gonna dance? The cop said in an affected Nellie voice. "C'mon. Let me see you dance. Show me your little girly dance." The cop sneered.

"But we're in heels, officer, and the ground is soft and muddy." Iona tried to reason.

"I SAID FUCKIN' DANCE!"

"Well ladies, since this officer seems to be in charge, the kick line at the finale," Iona directed without diverting her gaze from the officer's face.

Natalie stood frozen to the spot.

Linking arms, Fulla gave Natalie a tug. "Come on, Natalie. Now's not the time for a panic attack. Let's dance."

The ladies began a complicated box step, arms linked, and smiling brightly. Natalie walked the steps through but never lifted her eyes from the ground. As the women neared the end of their routine, they each in turn hopped on one foot and kicked up with the other. In her fright, Natalie kicked up too high, lost her footing and landed on her rear, sending one very large blood red high heel shoe soaring through the air. The heel struck hard between the officer's eyes. He hit the ground like a bag of stones.

"Oooh, girl, look what you did," Fulla said, stepping forward to examine the still body.

"Wow," said Deb, "I bet you couldn't do that again if they paid you."

Iona crouched down beside the prone figure and felt his wrist and jugular for a pulse.

"Well, you didn't kill him, anyway." She said.

"What a shame," Fulla sighed "Maybe you got a hammer somewhere and we could really drive that sucker home. Sort of like a calling card. Officer left with a stiletto sticking out his forehead."

"Oh my God! Oh my God! What am I gonna do?" Natalie wailed.

"He's just unconscious. You knocked him out cold." Deb offered.

"I got mud all over the back side of my dress." Natalie sobbed, twisting her torso to observe the damage.

"Girl, you got bigger problems than that," Fulla offered. "You just done knocked out a cop!"

"I wha-?" Natalie started and looked up from her contortion.

"You just damn near killed Captain Asshole here." Fulla explained. "Girl, I'm glad I'm not in your heels."

Natalie stood upright and stared at the prone uniformed figure in silence. She stood there in silence for half a minute and just stared. Then she began to breathe heavy and her face began to contort in rage. Her muscles tensed and her fists began to clench open and shut. And then with a yell that racked her soul, she thrust forward and began kicking and beating the unconscious figure. It took all three companions to pull her off the cop. Her wig was hanging off the side of her head and her make-up was smudged and streaking down her cheeks. She was panting and drooling and glaring at the officer. It took several minutes before the others felt they could release their hold on their companion.

And even then they stood between her and her victim.

"C'mon, Natalie. I'm sure we can find a new dress in the trunk which will fit you for tonight," Iona offered.

"What we gonna do with suckwad here?" Fulla asked.

"Leave him," Iona said over her shoulder. " I say we fix Natalie up, get the car going again, and just leave the asshole lying where he is."

Deb walked over to the police cruiser and removed the keys from the ignition. She inhaled deeply and threw the keys as hard as she could into the nearby trees.

Natalie stood with her fingers folded, looking over at the body lying on the grass.

"C'mon, dear, strip." Iona directed as she began peeling through dresses and wigs. "We don't have much time. Here's one that will do you justice. Just don't bend over too much or the seams will split out."

Natalie stood staring at the cop while Iona unzipped the dress. Iona held out the new cream-colored chiffon and lace dress but Natalie didn't take it. She seemed to gain some inner strength, stood taller, and a determined look began to harden her face.

"Girls, I have an idea." She said.

The ladies had traveled several miles down the road before the officer awoke from his injury. His head ached and there was a severe pain behind his left eye. His face felt thick and greasy and he pulled his hand up to rub his eyes. Long red fingernails poked his eyelids. He looked down at his hands sticking out of lacy chiffon sleeves. He stood up and staggered to the car mirror, tripping as the high heels stuck into the soft dirt. Sitting in the patrol car driver's seat, he adjusted the mirror. His face was made up in thick pancake make-up. His lips were a bright aqua and his head was covered with a very tall Nancy Sinatra bouffant wig. To his horror he discovered the wig, along with the nails and the cream-colored chiffon dress had been super glued to his body.

His scream startled several roosting birds into the dark night sky.

By Richard Muto

Lost and Found

"Ladies and gentlemen, I wish I had better news for you. But we are facing a storm that most of us have feared. I do not want to create panic. But I do want the citizens to understand that this is very serious, and it's of the highest nature."

--Mayor Ray Nagin, New Orleans.

From his perch on the back of the helicopter, Chaney Harrison scanned the perimeter of New Orleans. This was nothing like Iraq – these were our own; they needed saving. A city barely above water, a city screaming for help.

The whirling shrieks of the blades that kept his MH-53 airborne had grown dull, muffled by earplugs, subdued by familiarity. After six years as a pararescueman in the United States Air Force, Chaney's filter had grown finely tuned – he heard everything, just not all of it went through.

Then, he saw it. Immediately, Chaney was on the line. "We oughta make another pass, I got a lone litter out here," he called into the microphone. Even in these unusual circumstances -- a time defined by the drowning, the missing, and the helpless -- *this* was not normal. From 1,000 feet, Chaney could make out its outline immediately. This didn't feel right, not out there alone in the grass-covered field. Sure, it was a common, the object itself, but not alone, not after Katrina.

A litter, in Air Force terms, is a long wire basket braced by aluminum poles that run down the length and along the sides. From the aluminum poles extend various straps, designed to attach the litter to ambulance, helicopter, whatever. Problem was, this litter, sitting in the middle of this field, wasn't attached to anything nor being held by anybody. They'd have to make another pass, assess the situation. Chaney stayed calm -- *it was probably nothing.*

As they descended upon the field, Chaney took in the situation. This city, a mere day ago, ran like a clock. Sure, the time may have been a bit off and a few kinks may have developed in its mechanical inner workings, but the thing ran. Now, looking at the flooding, the destruction, you couldn't even get it started. Every piece had been broken, individually and collectively, and the clockmaker was nowhere to be found. *God*, he hoped, *let there be no one in that litter.*

***

In the year 2000, on the heels of an eye-opening wilderness awareness retreat in the jungles of Duvall, WA, Chaney Harrison could have never imagined himself a soldier. All he knew then, much as he truly understands now, was his love for nature -- a raw, burning desire telling him this, *this* is where you belong. Held back initially by the familiar issues of money and circumstance, Chaney finally saw his life permanently changed in the strangest of all places, The Gainesville Public Library.

It was on this day, much like any other, with this book, unlike any other, that Chaney's life would be changed forever: *So That Others May Live: The True Story of the PJs, the Real Life Heroes of the Perfect Storm* by Jack Brehm & Pete Nelson. Chaney read Jack Brehm's story – a heroic rescue set to the backdrop of one man's choice to devote his life in the pursuit of other's safety. To Chaney, the job of a pararescueman, or PJ, was just that: a job, but one that would provide him with everything he'd dreamed of: the outdoors, a true challenge, and decent money. First and foremost, the outdoors. He was sold.

***

Staring from the helicopter, Chaney was overwhelmed by heat; sweat cascaded from his thick brow, past the stubble obscuring his soft face and into the flooded city below. A weatherman would later that night report a high of 90 degrees, although no one would really listen. New Orleans may have been the nightly news for the rest of the world, but for those within city limits, a slightly more pressing issue took precedent.

The helicopter sunk to the ground, particles of dust flying up from beyond the grass. Chaney raced off the ramp and made his way towards the litter, his eyes squinting through the wind and the sun. The litter wasn't flat – it had mounds, valleys – it was a human body. Hovering over the litter, Chaney unfurled the top of the blanket – a face. A human body, alone in the field, forgotten.

Chaney immediately called for backup, as he continued to uncover the woman. Frail, old, probably in her mid-70's, she was unresponsive. He looked for a reaction, anything to indicate consciousness beyond the beating pulse his fellow officer had just announced. *Why was she left here? What if he hadn't seen her? Would anyone?*

***

Had things gone his way, as they generally did, Chaney wouldn't be here right now, not flying over this particular field. While at his base in Hurlburt Field, FL, two days prior on the morning of August 25th, 2005, Chaney anticipated this disaster in the making. By that point, Katrina had already torn through the Bahamas and made its way toward Florida with 80-mile-an-hour winds, reportedly killing nine and forcing the state of Florida to declare a state of emergency. Nine was just the beginning, Chaney understood all too well. He couldn't just sit by, passive.

Approaching the senior officer in his unit, Chief Master Sergeant Hoye, Chaney attempted to reason. He exclaimed, "We're the closest ones to the site, we're ready to fly. They need our help." The officer, without a second's hesitation, looked up from his papers and replied, "There is no identified need for the pararescue skill set in New Orleans right now." Over the officer's left shoulder, Chaney watched the TV: a pararescue team from as far away as New York or Arizona was cutting into a roof of a house with a chainsaw. *No identified need*, Chaney thought, *really?*

***

Carrying the litter back onto the ramp that lay ready into the back of the helicopter, Chaney's team tried to find that perfect balance of tempo, speed and haste. It is said that in times of unparalleled stress, man reverts back to his highest level of military training -- the mind stops thinking and acts on simple, animalistic instinct. Chaney had been trained for this, so he acted. If his gut could get him home safely from three tours in Iraq, it would save this woman. It had to.

Soaring back into the sky, the helicopter made a straight shot for the airport, specifically designed to handle causalities of this nature. Chaney looked up from his unresponsive patient and out over New Orleans. The Big Easy, people used to call it. Home to Louis Armstrong, jazz and careless Mardi Gras pleasure. Right now, it was anything but easy.

He had been here before, in this city. Roughly one year ago, he had attended a two-week training module in New Orleans driving with the local ambulances, refreshing and reviewing his medical training, all part of the job.

From this aerial point of view, Chaney saw so many landmarks he'd used a year earlier to orientate himself through the city's winding streets. Things were different now, distorted and sour. He remembered the streets he'd navigate on his way to work. Flooded. The hospital he had dropped the wounded at. Flooded. Even the on ramp for the I-10 highway that brought him in and out of the city. Flooded. It was surreal, the whole thing, but there was no time to take that in. There was a woman aboard his helicopter who needed saving. "These things I do, so that others may live." The Code of the Air Rescueman, it rang through his mind. Not in a conscious, forefront-of-thought kind of way, just there, so engrained in his being, driving all action, advancing all thought.

This poor woman would be OK, she had to be. *So that others may live.* They dropped her at the New Orleans Memorial Hospital and flew unceremoniously back up, into the sky. This was just the sixth hour of the first day. There would be so many more, wounded, unresponsive, and unwilling to leave their homes.

Chaney Harrison never found out the woman's name or what happened to her. He flew for five more days, carrying roughly 400 to safety in the process. He recalls the words of his commanding officer, "There is no identified need for the pararescue skill set in New Orleans right now." It could have been more, so many more.

By the end, 705 people were reported missing, 1,836 people dead.

By Alex Dobrenko

The Night Shift

Reading on my screened porch in an old wicker arm chair under a fifties' goose-neck floor lamp, I look up at the loud "wonk" of a nearby night heron — the porch my cave as I peer into the dark, and listen, and scent the night river. I'm focused on the small splashes of snapper blues chasing bait, when deep "huffs" direct my attention to two huge raccoon figures in the half light from the lamp a few feet from the porch. One turns and ambles around the side of the porch and then returns with two pre-teens.

Three of them amble away and out to my dock to clean up after the gulls afternoon blue crab feast. But one youngster has noticed me and comes over and props himself up with his front legs against the screen for a better look. After a bit, the other young one, chewing on a big blue crab shell, comes back to check on his sibling. Then all four gather, march down to the end of my wall, climb down to the little beach, and continue their nightly neighborhood round.

Ten minutes later a loud "hooooo" from my big American cherry startles me. Barred owl! Busy night.

By Richard V. Travisano

Precambrian Predecessors

Primordial organisms (purportedly and strictly based on my cumulative yet quite limited fount of knowledge gleaned from two score and ten years dawn to dusk personal fin de siecle episodes) lack any semblance of conscious awareness!

As a measure of what we (as the collective intelligence of Homo Sapiens) deem to be supreme mental acuity to comprehend the mind boggling concept of biological evolution from whence unicellular entities manifested into the vast differentiation of life in general and each individual man, woman and child in particular, I as an ordinary male mortal human being born within the latter half of twentieth century (Anno Domini before the advent of fettuccini) as a member of said genus and species now try to pontificate and understand the billions of years that elapsed and transpired from that initial incarnation of terrestrial events (perchance even originating from one or more stray cosmic objects) the barest essence of that schema quantified as existence (which incorporated random combinations and permutations moderated via the survival of fittest theoretical proposition) essentially conspiring to promulgate a barely discernable genetic connection that over millions of millennia later traced little electrical arcs that spanned the microcosmic gaps between the axons and synapses constituting the definitive lineage extant within said writer of these words.

[Understand this rather circumlocutious convoluted schema/theme thus far? Me neither! Ha!]

No particular rhyme or reason constitutes this personal intent to apprise and self actualize the vast (some might say utterly impossible) task to take stock of basic trappings percolating in so called primordial ooze (an incomprehensible number of billions of years in the distant past) which natural laboratory nearly comprising the entire planet earth harbored critical and essential atomic and/or molecular composition eventually distilling original progenitors inhabiting the incredibly varied animal and plant world.

Quite impossible for me as a non-scientific (yet contemplative, introspective and philosophical) person to gauge the innumerable eons and epochs that passed with little or no measurable alteration nor modification extant within that brew (vintage forever unknown) containing the rawest components identified as living forms!

A gross hunch prompts this layman to hypothesize the passage of imponderable blocks of time whereby a condition of stasis prevailed. Although it is difficult to understand what natural forces and processes set in motion a chain reaction that unleashed profound explosions (most likely registered as imperturbable repercussions within the salty brine) that instigated punctuated equilibrium.

Once the watery expanse (more pointedly isolated and specific pockets within the infant seas) housed these very tentative (nor to mention vulnerable) kernels, the elements at large (in my amateur opinion) contributed a slightly more favorable climate to allow, enable, promote a coalescence of greater amalgamation and assimilation among the invisible amorphous precursors to become far flung fauna and flora.

It is impossible (for an average occupant of this third rock from the sun) to assess the ambient chemical solution(s) that served as distillery for gradual trials and tribulations that unbridled compounds developed, which tandem mergers (possibly the very first leveraged buyout offerings -- with primitive venture capitalists) insinuated subsequent exponential occurrences granting increased infiltration among more complex units.

Prestigious professionals (at the pinnacles of their careers) possess far greater capacity and knowledge to explain undulations and variations that affected and brought about jolts, which factors (possibly atmospheric and aquatic) loosed and/or unleashed the tectonic prowess to burst into spectrum of life! Kingdoms distinctly qualified as either animal or plant inhabitants made way to this formative birth (day) of pseudo kinetic energies!

These earliest hosts to occupy the warm saline hydrosphere were more or less at the mercy of oceanic currents! They lacked deterministic criteria, but somehow (due as some might ascribe to divine intervention) devised appurtenances to augment replication.

This propensity to duplicate (offspring in an asexual manner) retained the legacy of core nucleic record. Simultaneous within each somewhat unique band or clump of miniscule flotsam and jetsam occurred the fluke symbiotic relationship that abetted greater manifestation of marine based denizens to populate suitably temperate oceans.

If this one deep thinker could interpolate and postulate per the view (with proper scuba gear and functional time travel machinery), he might be privy to behold an argot of chimerical dust-mote like shapes and sizes presenting a myriad kaleidoscopic, scintillating display of utmost breath-taking beautiful sight across the glistening miasma!

In truth, not one living soul ever experienced the microscopic hybrids, which concoctions of chance, fate and Mother Nature held the gamut of diversification within primitive coils and strands of DNA. Such latent potential forecasting (hundreds if not thousands of millennia in the future) the exotic and varied jumble offered up by the creative powers thriving in the organic, nutrient rich baths at some juncture in the space/time continuum spawned the era for substantial life to illustrate the subterranean expansive vistas!

Many pages, chapters and more accurately volumes, recorded via the hand of said universal creator (for no one to read nor see) the veritably unchanging drama that predominated across the ideally supercharged wetlands.

This lapse of eons (manifold lengthier than the dawn of civilization until this present twenty first century after the death of Jesus Christ) incomprehensible! Now try to imagine (an exercise in futility and nearly beyond the realm of possibility), these nascent nodules of nuclear nectar keeping intact within a Byzantine cellular paradigm for aforementioned span.

Numerous descriptive words such as indecipherable, ineluctable, inscrutable frequently rack and reverberate within my self-provoked mind when pondering such awesome notions. Just like every other bipedal creature happenstance brought into this world, I too contemplate questions about the spark that triggered the onset known as the spectrum of biosphere.

A personal manuscript of low research caliber perhaps conveniently quantified as fictional, improper and impolite for such stream of consciousness musings to attest as true, when little or no expertise (nor discrete or specific arcane knowledge) provides a privilege to claim authenticity and veracity.

This exposition of feelings, ideas and thoughts pertaining to the age-old question (from whence many religious belief systems sprung) only yields to the private domain lodged within the psychic makeup of this here one and only individual, who for reasons and rhymes unbeknownst to himself, suddenly entertains such an awesome concept and only wishes to capitalize on some literary skill to organize such sentiments into cogent paragraphs.

Damn near impossible to capture infinitely occurring poetic flashes of insight and queries that flit to and fro within the center of thinking and I realize this essay to represent a poor approximation of the vibrant jungle of prose that beckons to be carefully trod with a custom made scythe.

Lest an elusive prey escape (born from an overactive imagination), the return to a former point of existential pontification (vetted in the vat a can) will be brought back with a gentle massage to scalp to invigorate the dozing rapscallions, which fire up the axons and neurons.

This mind bending exercise to scrutinize the seething hospitable cauldron harboring the seeds of genesis, which reacted favorably to the ramifications in such fecund brew once again entertained more so as a way to while away leisure minutes and also perhaps to receive some commendable feedback (in the form of monetary remuneration) and subsequent publication.

Just to make clear once again, I embark on a rather exceptional task to organize bombardment of ruminations ricocheting (like a miniature super ball or two) within the gray matter in the cranium otherwise known as the brain.

Difficult if not downright impossible to codify in some clear and logical manner present assault pertaining to an unexpected preoccupation (not yet associated as obsessive/compulsive behavior) about realm affiliated as the eminent domain of intelligentsia filling the ranks and file of scholarly professors. I do not purport to excel nor outflank prestigious personages who spent extensive years examining biota (mostly thru advanced computer technology), but merely intended to compile an essay based on a current fount of knowledge resorting to my own insight into the commingling of events that brought forth this awesome zoological maelstrom.

Those most learned and smartest experts (who earned the right to belong to selective academic circles) dedicated to search for some clues holding the secrets per supreme mystery probably also experience bafflement and stymied investigations. Not for me to challenge nor trespass their doctrinal thesis substantiated by ample footnotes. No!

A peculiar frenzy holds extreme (yet harmless) fascination to explain in some understandable fashion my view of this schema signaling stratification from sparse sporadic (and spotty) globules (no doubt mere specks) giving rise to the abundant hierarchy of life.

In truth, an analysis of myself (which composite includes idiosyncrasies, nuances and quirks to list a few personal characteristics) accidentally led to this expanded scope to consider the history of mankind and of course womankind.

A chocolate swirl of intrigue motivates self-discipline epitomizing a quest to understand aspects inherent since birth and/or appearing later since a newborn.

Circumspection about entire ancestry might never be feasible, but this mental stretch could possibly offer a glimmer of present trials and tribulations by glimpsing back in the remote past. Without obedience to stated precedents and protocols and objection against poring over tombs in the reference section of libraries, I do bias this epistle and undermine the believability of numerable statements.

Claim to fame not the aim of this yahoo! None of these words ought to be accepted as the gospel according to Matthew Scott!

Each and every sentence (from beginning to end of manuscript) to be read as fictionalized fact. I sought some salvation from exploring journey within to yield a product that offers cleansing of soul. Psychic angst riddles (like Swiss cheese) mindset of an ordinary guy, which plague possibly a collective weakness woven (like a delicate and fine thread) since that faint, first tapestry strand coaxed from a miraculous spate of incidents.

Now let me get back to brass tacks and return to the former epistemological focus of this treatise!

Flourish of material approximating a masquerade of organisms occurred early in the geologic history of this oblate spheroid frequently alluded as the emerald in the sky!

Rather than ascribe any particulars to this concept (since no intent goads me to compromise the vested establishment nor interest of the scientific community) I affirm that way back thru the fog and mist of space/time continuum unbridled activities ushered the ideal milieu to groom the physical environment for a plentiful outburst of bio-diversity to materialize.

At some indiscriminate occasion fantastic forces affected a propensity for quiet explosion to rock the firmament. Still, no definitive entities would be visible in the two hydrogen atoms plus one oxygen atom special elixir!

Many tens of thousands of sheets contained in the epic writ large (and small) via (some might vouchsafe by benevolent hand of a benign creator) must be flipped until a more robust sample exemplifying a similar facsimile labeled animal or plant identified.

Here and there one might discern the features resembling so named simplest (in terms of cellular structure) beings that could very well represent our earliest progenitors!

As one fast-forwards (in the figurative sense of course) additional, these leafs from metaphorical copious text, a noticeable proliferation of multifarious (not to mention mellifluous) critters dot the landscape.

As if by abracadabra magic or sleight of hand, a bounty of teeming hosts luxuriated in glorious mornings. Most if not all these characters thrived in the lavish liquid lowlands.

Proletariats by default, a small minority would emigrate to the lush, solid and vegetation covered ground. Such segue-way from aquatic to terrestrial habitués entailed passage of a good many hundreds of thousands more revolutions or Earth round the sun.

An uptick in the in the energetic flux spurred logarithmic poufs and more radical pulses and waves as an after affect of the Godlike wizard wand, which wrought prestidigitatious preponderance of nubile buds and pods beckoning rambunctious awakening diadems to expand in quantity.

Gregarious landlubbers soon slithered from the ooze, which if fast forward photography was present would portray a migration of wormlike wonder-kinds.

Once again, I pledge allegiance to ask forgiveness in straying from any factual formulations and also to take poetic/prosaic license in stipulating such archaic scenarios.

Such literary promiscuity gives leeway to supplement this semi valid tale with exaggeration and hyperbole!

By Matthew Scott Harris

The Raven and the Sparrow

Running, it feels like I am always running, running from family, friends, running from everything and nothing at the same time. It's all I can do, constantly changing faces in the blink of an eye, my masks are endless, as they are ripped off and disregarded. The skin makes a hallow slice of a sound as it falls to the floor lifeless. Its empty eyes and void emotions are left in the dust like the alias that follows it. I have so many faces, so many names, that even if they think they are close to grabbing my hand another falls and replaces that grip with air. Another dark ally and another crime to attend to, but the phantom never wanders far. She stands above the streets as her eyes shoot out from behind a dark mask, my mask. I can be the villain, I can be the savior. I am the victim, and I can be the convicted. Yet with angelic speed I continue down the street with large black wings that fade in the darkness leaving a single feather behind. A feather that can be cherished or can be detested as trash but it's still there. Sitting on your soul like a broken piece of glass sits in a wound waiting to be ripped out, but never really thrown away. Though now the battle seems to be in vain.

I run and yet they always manage to catch me. Their hands reach farther then most imagine, despite the fear, the pain, the anger; I can never run fast enough. I am stuck in a bird cage too small for my large wing span. Tight and confined, all my beliefs, ideas, opinions they are squashed into my mind and held there by large solid gold bars. Bars which lack the room to stretch, they are firm and cold like the minds of those who smile so brightly around me. It's a pretty facade, just like all the smiles and the friendships that seem too good to pass up. Yet, once they get just close enough to make you believe their sanctuary the cage remains. Everyone still stares in awe but never move forward to undo the latch and open the doors. I wait, and wait...to finally have the open arms pulled me from the cage that I was placed in. All the arms are open and wide but maybe I am stilling running. I shy away from the kid touches, wincing from the possible chance of betrayal if I get to close. I fear the firm hand that seems to smack the kindness away and leave nothing but a broken mirror of memories of what was there.

Being alone is always the final result. No matter how many smaller birds come and rest in my fake gold cage, in the end they all fly away. Leaving me nothing but the memory of the fleeting love, the touch, which lingers on my breast where they rested. Some return again, while others keep their distance and watch from afar. Never again do they get close enough to touch, to hold, and to love. They know me, they understand that I am there, but none have the courage to cut away the cage from my cramped black wings. Is it my fault? Do I push them away? The friends never stay long enough for me to figure it out.

Running, run, run, and run...it's a constant method. In the end though, even if the cage door was opened, would I have the courage to receive the open arms? Would I fit loaded with all my fears and distrusts though the small open door? I have grown so used to the cramped lonesomeness that it seems almost a shame to leave it alone, for something less familiar. Yet I sit like a wide eyed child, watching those who aren't caged sing, no matter how much they sing of things ignorant and childish, I long to be the song bird. I have no voice to sing, it's rough, and hoarse from the age old ideas that burn at my throat longing to be spoken. If I did sing, would I sing like the other birds? No, I already know that the mature tone of my voice would stand out, and once again I would be placed in this cage. So I sit. My knees to my chest, my back arched uncomfortably against the bars that confine me. Will I be able to stand when it finally comes time or have I forgotten what it feels like to stand tall and proud? Have I lost the only trait that makes me a bird? I no longer remember how to fly.

By Alexandra Epervary

Sasha vs. The Red Vests

*"'48 minutes for the next 48 years of our lives. I say we go out there and we leave it all out on the field. We got the rest of our lives to be mediocre, but we have the opportunity to play like Gods. **Let's be heroes**."*

--*Varsity Blues* Trailer, as seen at the Dobrenko Household
Saturday, February 13th, 1999

I laid on the burnt-red fibers of the family room carpet, the closing words of the *Varsity Blues* trailer still resonating in my ears: *Let's be heroes.*

Within seconds, I was up, sprung from the carpet and sprinting towards the kitchen, a plan of action slowly solidifying with every bouncy step. Today, I'd be the hero.

This idea, the third of the day, was a thousand times better than my previous two of the day, and equally as difficult.

Idea One and Idea Two went hand in hand this morning, the first a delicious strawberry shortcake, good for its taste, and, immediately following, the second -- a glass of coke good both for cleaning my mouth and inducing my sugary, jittery state of speech for the day.

I nearly knocked the glass over, still half-full, as I ran into the kitchen where Mom was using her favorite weapon, *the metal mallet of death*, to pulverize pink slabs of white meat into their flat, pancake looking alter-egos. She was cooking *beetoks*, my favorite food in the world, something I would explain to any of my American friends in the only way I knew how: *massa s iyichka –* meat with egg.

I had to scream to be heard over the *whap whap whap* of the mallet.

"Mom, I'm soOoOo *bored!* Can we go to the movies!?"

Usually, this was a simple formality – the question that would necessitate a "yes" response. Mom would oblige, and I would run to the phone and call the voice who sounded just like the men in suits with greasy hair who sold cars on TV, but more automated. He would tell me, after what always felt like a very impolite explanation of the theater's hours and other things I already knew, about the movies in the theater and what times *Varsity Blues* would play.

The one problem was, this movie wasn't just any movie. This wasn't *Toy Soldiers.* This wasn't *Can't Hardly Wait.* And this certainly wasn't *Patch Adams.* In short, this wasn't PG-13. This was *Varsity Blues.* This movie was rated R.

Now visibly hesitant, Mom began her battery of questions, asking what the movie was about, why it would get this horrible Rating of R, and why they had to say all those *bad* words in the first place. I allowed this to continue for its necessary duration before explaining in my now perfected slow, calm demeanor, "Mom, you watch Rated R movies all the time without knowing it. It's really not a big deal, OK? So can we go?"

***

The red snake of velvet that would guide us to the ticket stand appeared clearly through the window of the Sharon Movie Theater. I led the way, followed begrudgingly by Mom. By that point in our slow induction into the American way of life, she had begun to appreciate movies, or at least pretended to for the sake of her one and only child. I was still, and always would be, her little Sasha.

When we moved, a strange man who didn't know me or Mom or Dad told us that boys aren't called Sasha here and that my name should be Alexander. Ever since, I've gone by Alex to everyone but Mom and Dad.

Approaching the counter, I acted as confident as my less than average height and cheeks puffed full of strawberry shortcake would allow. Today, I'd have to be American Alex.

"Hi, one for *Varsity Blues,* please."

The red-vest looks at me. His eyes take less than a second to take it all in before darting at my mom, "He isn't 17, is he?"

I interrupt, hoping to explain the simple, yet often misunderstood understanding of the wording that defines an R rating. My English is strong, my arguments reasonable & logical.

Mom's white teeth grin back at the vest while I feverishly pitch my case; she wishes she could be back with her mallet, making food for the week.

The guard responds as if the entire response was ready before I even began speaking, "Yeah, I mean, I get what you're saying, it's just there is really nothing I can do. Rated R means that, 'Children under 17 are not allowed to attend R-rated motion pictures unaccompanied by a parent or adult guardian'. That's it. End of story, kid."

Bah! Foiled by the vest. What was American Alex, the *man,* to do?

After a brief, private discussion with Mom, we decide that I can just see a movie with her that is not Rated R and, before I know it, we had bought two for *Message in a Bottle.* Yeah, I couldn't force her to see a movie about high school football, it just wasn't right, but *Message in a Bottle?* I'm a 13 year old boy on the verge of manhood and I'm going to see a movie about love and bottles in the ocean. Awesome.

This cannot be the way the story ends, it just can't, I think, as we waltz past the popcorn stand. I ponder absentmindedly about drowning out the bottle love with a bucket of salty popcorn, and then, out of nowhere, another idea slowly presents itself. *No,* I think, *not yet.*

We get in and sit. I try to withstand the pain of this romance, watch some previews about love and humor, classic PG-13 tropes, until I simply cannot take it any longer. It is time to employ the deadly fourth plan.

I begin a quick discussion with mom, confidence overwhelming, and she allows me to leave, understanding that today, I truly must be what I am born to be: a hero.

I walk back past the first red vest of the day, maintaining with the poise and precision my aura of adult. As long as he doesn't see me, I'm fine. I had earlier scouted the door for *Varsity Blues* – at the complete opposite end of the theater.

***

I hear the door slam behind me. I'm in. Success, Freedom, All of it! I am...Rated R. I am a hero.

I sit and watch the previews, most of a level I had never seen before. The swears fly like never before – *Fuck* this, *Shit* that – each new cuss an unknown note, together composing the melodious tone of adulthood previously unimaginable by little Sasha, today heard by Alexander, leader of men.

The movie starts, and almost immediately, I realize why I shouldn't be here. A girl -- the popular, pretty one -- has just come on screen wearing a bikini made not from any cloth I've ever seen before, but instead the creamy, white fluff of whipped cream. Three cherries cover the especially bad parts of her. What was so bad about this, I thought? *Oh,* I realized, they're *going to have sex*. Weird.

I continued watching as Mox -- the football player with dreams of something bigger -- hung out with his friends, fought with his dad, and practiced his football, all of the activities I assumed were a normal part of the high school experience. This pretending wasn't too difficult within the all-black theater – I would stay silent when others stayed silent and laugh when others laughed. My voice, currently in the throws of a rather unpredictable battle with puberty, could not be counted on to maintain its newly found deep tone. It could, and would, squeal at any moment, revealing its high-pitched former self. This was unacceptable, my PG-13 identity could not be revealed to the other movie-goers, let alone the red-vested employee who had walked in a few minutes prior.

At the beginning of the movie, I kept meticulous track of that door's openings and closings, attributing each to either a fellow moviegoer buying snacks or using the bathroom. However, as soon as I saw the first red-vest enter I realized my neck's constant twisting and turning would need to cease immediately. Otherwise, I'd risk sending the blatantly insecure signal of a PG-13er, grounds for immediate removal *and* maybe even a stern talking to from police who would have no problem using some of the words I had become accustomed to with my viewing experience.

So, I stared at the screen straight ahead, watching even more intently with my beady, but not too beady eyes, calibrated to a perfect level of an interested, yet not too interested seventeen year old male.

Mox continued to fight, play, and kiss, and the swears continued to rain down in waves, though the only thing I could think about was that vest. *Where was he? Could I see him? Could he see me?* I began to crane my head back and to the right, ever so slowly. Slower and slower, turning, now 90 degrees away from the comic relief on screen, I could easily make out the red-vest, still and silent, staring at the screen. My heart was racing as I began my neck's slow rotation back to...

Wait! What the f---. What was that? What the hell was that light! At about thigh-level, in direct line with my eyes appeared from nowhere a bright circle of shining light.

Oh god. Heart is beating. Palms are sweaty. My whole body becomes rigid, slouching slow, slow and steady, so that the top of my head is no longer visible to those behind. *Just act cool. Don't move. Nice and still. Gah!*

I couldn't hold, I had to know what was going on; what the hell was he doing with that light. I turn completely, using my left eye to peep through the natural slit between the chairs.

Shit! He was checking someone else's ID. Oh god, they look scared. I could feel the puddles of water forming on the arm rests to which I now clung for dear life. Oh god, they're getting up, and, yep, they're leaving. They just got kicked out for being underage!

I was doomed. Sitting a few rows above the vest's current location, I had no idea what to do. I wanted, more than anything, to just scream for Mom or go back in time and take back that stupid third idea and just be happy with the first two but I couldn't, so I just lowered myself even more and more, sucking in my gut and straightening myself as much as possible to become one with the dark, plushy fabric fastened to the back of my seat. I could see the glow emanating from his flashlight now, swerving all over the room like a firefly on cocaine.

It was coming closer and closer, this firefly – the vest moving row by row, inspecting, and moving on. He was just one row away from me now. Stay rigid, stay hidden, I thought, as I closed my eyes for fear of what was to come next – his walking over, asking for my ID, taking me outside where inevitably the first red-vest would reveal my earlier ploy, call the police, and, worst of all, ruin *Message in a Bottle* for Mom.

Closer and closer the flashlight got, inches from me, moving closer and, boom! I felt it penetrate my closed eye-lids, turning the horrified darkness into even more petrified light. It was over; I was a hero no longer.
Wait, what? What's going on here? Do I feel darkness again? Is this a joke? Did the vest really just gloss past me? Did he mistake me for a 17 year old? Oh my god, he did. Success for Sasha! Sasha the Hero!

My mom met me in the lobby a few minutes after my movie's conclusion, her hands clutching a few crumpled tissues used to wipe the now puffy bags under her eyes where tears had been. I looked at those eyes, crying because of some message that I only could imagine, received by the transport of a bottle, and I realized how happy I was she wasn't crying about me, her son in jail for sneaking into a movie about football, whipped cream bikinis, and a lot of cussing.

"How was the movie?" she asks, as we walk past the unsuspecting vests and follow the velvet snake towards the door. Me, I respond, "I've seen better."

By Alex Dobrenko

Sausages

Her hands were in the photograph I held with both hands. When she got up she didn't say thank you, may I walk with you? Didn't say no. I held her hands, we walked a picture, the one they hid in your eyes. The more I look, the less I find. By the way, aren't you married?

She didn't say, won't you? Didn't say no! We did! Days were passing as the wind and nights were no longer than seconds. We were two lonely photos that the world wanted to expel from the album. Expelled! Don't believe it? Tonight when we're sleeping obverse in another photo. Pay that album a visit.

Open the fridge door in that shot and help yourself to whatever... Sorry! We only have sausages!

By Ali Abdolrezaei – Translated By Abol Froushan

Sky Blue

The Sky was mirror of buildings and streets, hollow of life and dead to anything. There were no faded blue or white puffs; those were now legends which marked the tails of the Grandparents to their children's children. To my people the sky was hazy, if you would call it a sky. It was void of life, not even the birds flew through it anymore. They hung low to the ground easing their way through the crowds of people who walked the musky and busy streets. People and Robot walked hand in hand, and lived a life that united both races. They complimented each other, aiding the other as needed. Every family had one. A person they called their own, cold oil blooded beings that carried nothing but programmed emotions. They were cold to touch, and conversation, the only moments they had life was when they smiled. Laughter was their only emotion, they felt no pain, no sorrow, and they hated no one, and loved all. The image of perfection, our perfection, or at least the image we thought was perfect. All their flaws could be fixed by a minor tweaking of screws or bolts that were masked under the flesh like skin they had on their bodies, my body.

I am one of the cold bloods, a being based on the image of a child god who sits in their shops and decided who was best to be given the life we live. Our god, if there is such a thing. They lived under the mirror sky that shields the blue from pictures, keeping all weather outside. The only thing that lived inside was man created. All organic objects had to be created by specialists, people of the past who lived off herbs and nature. Man now was messing with nature, cloning was something that happened more and more often. Life could be solved by a click of a button on a computer. Illness wasn't a threat anymore. Everything had a cure. Or at least we hoped that to be so. We gave everything we had to the Mirror Sky above our heads. It's a reminder of the world we created, and how we cast out everything that made the world full of life. The face we made and are forced to stare at every time we turn our eyes towards the empty void above our heads, my head.

Free will is something I've never had and probably never will. My life is controlled by wires and plugs that are hidden behind the flesh mask I get fixed every month or so, a flesh that if cut bleeds nothing and never heals, vacant of any fluid, vacant to life. I am like the world, empty of life and restrained to the will of the man god, my master, my life, my everything. They know little of the control they have over me and my people. Our minds cannot comprehend disobedience, nor do we understand rebellion. The only will we have is that embedded behind our eyes. They eyes that watch the red bloods live their lives like nothing is wrong. Which wake the world around us shrivel at the will of the people beside us, and the world being taken over by filth that clogs our lungs but we breathe. And with every inhale we take the eyes I was given see a little more, I am the worlds eyes. That watches everyone, the real image that everyone's eyes choose to see, my eyes.

We're always watching, seeing the nature reactions, what is acceptable and not to the world we live in, like a child learning manners from scratch. I am a child, a child stuck in the body already assigned for me. This is not my body, I have no solid form. I am a soul created by numbers placed in a vessel to be toyed with, mocked, and harbored, an image that the person who designed me created for a purpose, my purpose. That is if I have a purpose. Yet I like to believe that my purpose is to give everything else a reason to live. To show the red bloods the path to their success at my own expense.

It's a feeling that makes us almost feel the pounding of a nonexistent heart, the vital organ that makes us human. The heart of the millions my people aid every day, my heart.

By Alexandra Epervary

Snapshots of Our Family Trip to Aruba

Getting There

The plane's lifting off out of Atlanta now and I can feel the bubbles expanding in my ears. My sister's cuddled up next to me, already dozing off into her sinus-medicated sleep. The soft huffs of her breath are shoved out of my mind by the fluidic swell pulsating through my ear canal. Yawn. Yawn. Swallow. Swallow. And nothing. How will I ever make it through this flight with this water balloon moving around in my head?

I picked up this cold two days before our big family vacation to Aruba – two days. I've been healthy all year – survived the swine flu epidemic at school – and then Saturday night comes around and suddenly I'm awake with a migraine, a runny nose, and a stale, lumpy taste in the back of my throat. I looked in the mirror the next day to find a mucus-crusted face, swollen with exhaustion, and all I could think was 'who the hell did this to me?'

"Don't worry, the worst of it will probably be over before we leave," said my mom, but alas, here I am blowing my nose on this Delta napkin that came with my complimentary pretzels due to the fact that I've already run out of clean tissues. And there sits my mom, peacefully reading with her chin raised and her seatbelt securely strapped across her lap. Prim and proper are two words that come to mind when looking at her. For me, I'd think blowy and boogery.

My sister's mouth has fallen open in her drug-induced slumber; my dad's watching the romantic comedy dangling three rows ahead of him, without any headphones in his ears because he refuses to fully commit to any solitary activity; and my mom's lip is quivering over something 'riveting, touching, emotional!' in her book; I'm struggling to breathe, and we are all preparing to land in Aruba according to the pilot on the PA system.

The First Night

"Are you drinking tonight?" my mom asks.

"No, I don't think so."

"You can have one drink, it won't kill you."

"Mom, I'm sick!"

The drinking age is 18 here in Aruba, which seemed pretty exciting to me a week ago, but with my head still throbbing from the plane ride, the last thing I want is to feel tipsy.

We're sticking around our hotel tonight for a buffet and a Native Aruban dance show. It's been a rough day so far, so we're hoping the 'Eat what you can' buffet spread and music will lighten everyone's mood, particularly dad's. When we first arrived at our hotel, the clear blue ocean (or sea rather – weird!) was so breath-taking that my sister, my mom, and I couldn't wait to walk across the street and feel the toasty sand between our white, calloused and wintery feet. Unfortunately, within the five to ten minute time span that us females had wandered off, our room opened up and my dad had defiantly dragged off all of the suitcases to the room by himself and decisively left my mom's purse in the lobby unattended for her to retrieve herself. Luckily no wallets were stolen and the stunning scenery didn't fade while we were all caught in a momentary family blip of bitter words and confusion.

The food was what we needed. Mom claims to hate buffets, but here she comes with a second plate full of food.

"I'm not going to eat all of it, I just want to taste everything," she says. Ok, sure mom, but she did a little more than just taste the chicken skewers with peanut sauce or just try the seafood pasta. A-mazing. I ate like I had never seen meat and potatoes before in my life. Protein, fruits, nourishment, mmm, it was all so worth the long day of Biscoff cookies and cardboard pretzels the size of my thumbnail. Yes, my throat was still sore, but it was coated with barbecue sauce and mango juice.

The music started playing just after we had all filled our dessert plates. A bright white light clicked on to illuminate the stage and direct everyone's attention, but the light just so happened to be parallel to our heads and passed straight through our dinner table. All other tables were still dark and dignified as my sister shone suddenly bright, with her mouth wide open and a brownie hovering over that cavity. Someone working on the set must have recognized this uncomfortable situation, because the light clicked off only seconds later, making the whole moment seem very dramatic and terrifying: a flash of lightning and BOOM ! Girl eating cake! Then the mysterious darkness again. Other lights were manipulated so the show could begin.

Whistle. Whistle. Woot. Woot. This Aruban dance performance is not quite a kid friendly show. Three tall, magnificent dark-skinned women come out onto the stage ornamented in little more than beads and triangles of cloth and begin to bend and shake against their male counterparts. The dancing is fascinating, hypnotizing, but I think the majority of the crowd is far more entertained by the jiggle of the beads rather than the dance steps and movement. The father at the table next to us pokes his nose by mistake with his straw – case in point.

The men of the crowd have their entertainment, but we women are a little disappointed by the Aruban men in the show. They all wear bright orange, long pants and the best dancer is the one who looks thirteen years old. His hips twist rapidly around while his little orange butt shakes with an intensity and passion for the music that well exceeds the women's. I struggle to contain this overwhelming urge to burst out laughing before the next musical interlude. I'm trying to concentrate on the other dancers, but all I can see is that fanatical little orange blur in the corner of my eye.

And then comes the audience participation bit. The dancers disperse out into the crowd to sneak up in the dark behind their unsuspecting victims and pull them into the spotlight as stunned and vulnerable beings. Dad's sitting next to me with his hand viciously gripped around his Mai Tai, ready to use the glass as a weapon if necessary. I'm feeling oddly relaxed in my drowsy, sick state. Immune, I say to myself, surely they won't pick the sick girl, when here comes cha-cha boy, shaking his hips towards me.

"Would you like to dance?" he asks, already pulling out my chair and taking my hand.

Crap.

Bad day to wear a strapless bra. He dances circles around me and puts my female hips to shame – how does he move so fast? The whole population of the hotel is watching, including the most perceptive of all – my family! So I gather up some energy and attempt to compete with this little ball of fire. I lift up his arms and spin, smiling down at his face. I can dance too, little spunky boy. You and your salsa hips aren't putting me to shame. I pull him around and bump my hips up with every step. He follows me, but he looks concerned. I try to spin again, but he instructs me to hold onto his shoulder and follow him. 'Follow you?' I say to myself, 'that's no fun, I want to dance my own way – I'll be the only victim from the crowd who's not afraid to be up here!'

I'm in my own little sick, congested world up there, believing that everyone's looking at me, impressed by this random audience member that exhibits such talent! Dancing to my own tune, I fling myself and the frightened boy into another couple.

"Ooh, sorry," I say.

"Here follow me," the boy implores. "We're doing a dance."

He puts my arm decidedly around his shoulder again and moves me left then right, spin, and turn. We continue this pattern a few times over without bumping into any other dancers. I'm slowly realizing that this isn't a freestyle dance and everyone's doing the same steps in unison. Oops. Well how was I supposed to know?

"Now hold out your arms and shimmy like this," he says. My dress and bra begin to slide down at this point. In a very discreet fashion, I momentarily cease shimmying and drop my dance partner's hands to hoist up my dress and align my bra back into place. I take the boy's hands and begin to shake again with a lady-like smile to make up for all the embarrassment I've caused him. Still he seems pretty disturbed, grinning weakly and looking around at the crowd wondering why he had to pick me out of all these people.

The song goes on for far too long and the lights shine too bright on my sickened face, but my high-on-mucus state of mind wards off any embarrassment or shame I should have felt during the whole experience. I float back to the table like I have just stepped off a roller coaster – confused, disoriented, yet extremely elated. No idea what just happened.

Afterwards, our family heads back to our hotel room to pass out. They don't say much about the dance, so I'm a little concerned, but I blame their lack of praise on jet lag.

My parents sneak off into the bedroom – "Goodnight guys," they say. My sister and I frantically search for the other bed. There is none.

"Hey mom, where's our bed?" I ask.

Dad pokes his head out from the grand bedroom and points to something behind me. "Right there, that's it. Look underneath, a bed pulls out."

I have never heard of a trundle before in my life – had no idea such a thing existed, and let me say this: I hope to never cross paths with one ever again. It's a couch that has a dusty wooden-framed bed hidden beneath as a novelty, which can be pulled out and smiled at as a silly idea someone had, but in actuality should never be used by anyone. I thought I had the right idea choosing this roll-out part as my choice of sleeping apparatus, seeing as it most resembled a bed with a mattress and rectangular shape unlike the couch, but I was mistaken. The mattress on the trundle is stiff and unyielding and the structure is just low enough to the ground that all one breathes in at night is a combination of dust bunnies and mold.

Long night. At least dad's snores are muffled by the walls.

A Night Out on the Town

I woke up this morning as an old, grouchy man. The coughing began at four in the morning and hasn't stop till now. The sun is up and the parents are shuffling around, getting into their running clothes and sneakers so it must be around eight in the morning.

"Good morning, sweetie," my mom whispers.

Grumble. Grumble.

"Do you still want to get up and go for a walk on the beach?"

"My back hurts and my nose is stuffy and this trundle sucks."

My mom walks away to go about her business as if she's heard all she needs to.

"Mom, did you hear me?" I snarl.

"Yes, so I'm assuming you want to sleep in?"

I get up to drag my misery closer to my parents and let it curl up on their bed, whining audibly so they can't escape the frustration I feel. Dad splashes his forehead with water and mom applies make-up to her face, which makes no sense since she'll be sweating it off soon anyway.

"Mooom, I don't know what to do," I say.

She steps into the bedroom where I lay to grab her hair elastic. She continues to look everywhere except towards me and then gently says, "Well if you want to stay in this morning, stay in, or if you want to go for a walk, go for a walk. It's that simple."

I'm grumpy and every option sounds stupid, especially in that calm matter-of-factly voice. I decide to just close my mouth and wait for the day's events to soothe out my unjustifiable anger.

Dinner out tonight. We can't stick around the hotel forever so we decide to explore the downtown area of Aruba to see what life on the island is really all about. To heck with the high rise hotel strip – that's for stuck-up tourists, my dad says. We're an open-minded family and we're not afraid of a little taste of culture and experience.

"Oh, come on in guys! The bus driver says we can fit!"

Waiting at the bus stop, I assumed we'd be riding a city-type bus into town with a licensed bus driver and an isle with seats and windows, but my dad has flagged down what looks to me like one of the local's personal vans with a little sign attached to the top that says 'bus'. The white paint is chipped and scratched all along the side and the windows are tinted black, so all types of mischief and mayhem could be going on inside without the public eye knowing. Our fellow bus-stop lingerers stay back on the sidewalk as if they know better.

"Dad, are you sure you don't want to wait for the real bus?"

"What are you talking about? This is a bus." Yeah, according to the homemade sign glued to the roof – "Come on, there's people waiting inside."

And people there were indeed. My mom, my sister, and I squeeze together in the far back seat to avoid sitting next to the two scruffy men in the middle who are watching our dressed-up little family with an intensity that makes me wish I was in the habit of carrying pepper spray. The windows are cracked from the inside. My cushion has been gnawed on and mangled by a crazy person.

"For Christ sake," my mom whispers in my left ear, "I hope they let us out."

My sister's sitting unnaturally upright, avoiding as much contact with the interior of the 'bus' as possible, while my dad smiles, looking out at the boarded-up houses and stray dogs with a casual gaze as if this is the usual route into town. Fortunately, he doesn't try to strike up a conversation with the other passengers; he can give up his pride for good sense to some extent at least.

To my relief and my mom's disbelief, the van driver takes us into town and lets us out safely, but I don't know if the downtown area of Aruba is any safer. Dark corners and rough bars surround us, so we nonchalantly scrabble up the nearest stairs to a Mexican restaurant that overlooks the street. We had set out looking forward to fresh Aruban fish dinners and tropical dishes, but fajitas and salsa sound good for tonight considering the circumstances.

Drinks are served, our second basket of chips and salsa arrive, and we are feeling pretty comfortable. From the height of this balcony, we can see the darkened sea with the sprinkle of light reflected from the night sky above. My dad talks about the Milky Way and where it would be up there if only the lights from the world weren't so bright. The cheesy Acapulco music fades into the background as we all look up in the appropriate spot where dad's pointing, but I know we're all thinking about different things. With the endless black sky for our anxious eyes to rest in, our minds are free to flow clear and wide. I can usually take a guess at what my family's thinking about on a daily basis, but at this moment, we are our own secret people.

And then it all shatters.

woooOOOP!
woooOOOP!
woooOOOP!

Someone's car alarm goes off just below the balcony of the restaurant. People look around anxiously for someone to blame. Whose car is that? Stand up you jerk, we know you're around here somewhere! Everyone looks equally annoyed and confused. The owner of the car isn't here.

woooOOOP!
woooOOOP!

"Ah! How annoying!" my sister says. She sucks down her margarita to try to muffle the noise.

woooOOOP!
woooOOOP!

The restaurant shrinks with each shriek and suddenly all the other tables of people seem uncomfortably close to ours. I blow my nose on someone else's napkin by mistake and stick an unwrapped straw in my soda.

woooOOOP!
woooOOOP!

Mom mumbles something.

woooOOOP!

"WHAT?" the rest of us shout.

She's laughing now with a tortilla chip held weakly in her hand. The noise is deafening, but the squeaks at the end of each explosion of her laughter are still audible over the racket. She catches her breath and tries again, "I SAID DO YOU GUYS WANT TO STAY HERE FOR DESSERT?" and that's when the town clock begins to chime in and we all lose it.

woooOOOP! Ding dong!

woooOOOP! Ding dong!

The restaurant has turned into a circus of zany noises and crazy people. A man enraged by the madness begins mimicking the car alarm, shouting back at the hunk of metal that is so concerned with being robbed. The women try to ignore all the commotion and enjoy their fried ice cream while the kids look around enthralled by the chaos, anxiously awaiting what disastrous event might take place next. My sister hunches her neck down and then wiggles her head up to the sound of the alarm – woooOOOP! Over and over again her head snakes up in the air, impersonating the obnoxious noise with a goofy expression on her face, summing up the whole atmosphere of the vacation so far – crazy.

Thankfully, the noises stop in time for mom to order dessert.

De Palm Island

Banana boat rides mean business.

We have planned a half-day trip to De Palm Island today from 10:00 to 2:00, which requires a bus to pick us up down the road from our hotel at 9:30 a.m. for a fifteen minute bus ride followed by a ten minute boat ride to reach our destination, all somehow adding up to a 6:30 a.m. wake-up call in dad's mind. Three hours to brush our teeth and put on bathing suits? Twenty-one years of having to deal with my sister's tedious make-up and shower routines has left my dad scarred.

"It's too early. Wake us up in an hour," she says.

"No, get up now or you'll make us late."

My dad's a sincere, generous man – when elementary teachers asked me to write about someone I admire, his face usually came to mind first – but when my dad gets angry, he holds nothing back. A ticking time bomb he can be at times, taking in the bothers of his life quietly with little more than a tick until one of them finally sets him off and everything explodes in one outburst of rage. Other times, like today, he's a mine field, ready to blow up at every wrong move someone makes. We all make it to the bus stop early – he is pleased – but we are too early. My nose starts to drip from the waiting.

I cough and something blobs up into my mouth from my throat and it's gross and I have to spit it out. There are other families gathered around us, smiling and admiring the palm trees and early morning breeze, who probably wouldn't be very pleased if I spit out this jelly glob on the sidewalk near them. Desperate I look for a trashcan. I can only see one and it's the awkward kind with a push flap on the side – too much could go wrong there with gravity and angles. I can't alert my parents with this goo sitting on my tongue so my only option is to run to the bathroom through the lobby as quick as I can and make it back here before the bus arrives.

My mind sometimes fills in the spaces of my life where a song is needed: 'Run run Rudolph, you gotta spit that loogy out now! Run run Rudolph, before the bus makes it back to town!' I was amused until I heard the De Palm Island bus engine growling outside.

I sprint back outside, throwing acceptable social demeanor to the way side in order to get to my dad before his rage reaches its highest point. People are still boarding the bus, but my dad finds it necessary to wave his arms about and shout to the bus driver, "Hold on! We're waiting on one more person!"

Me.

A glare and a silent shove onto the steps of the bus is all he can tolerate giving to me at that moment. Every person on that bus watches me walk down the aisle. My cheeks are radiating from the eyes burning up at me from all sides. I am reminded of a time in my young life when my fed-up mother carried me out of a restaurant under her arm like a log and everyone in the dining room stared at us. I was younger then and could close my eyes if I wanted, but in this instance, the humiliation can't be avoided. It is a tense and quiet ride out to our day of fun.

Once we reach the island made up of beaches, snorkeling areas, water slides, open bars, and free buffets, my dad and I forget we were holding grudges.

Many of the tourists stand in awe, wondering where to start, but we have our minds set on one activity in particular – Banana boats! Banana boats! We pardon our way around slower families and rush down the dock to the front of the line.

Neither I nor any of the three members of my family have ever actually ridden a banana boat before. We have only seen them from the shore, way out in the ocean worming up and down behind a boat with people riding along, appearing to be enjoying themselves. Looks fun – I wonder if we'll get wet.

"Ok, everybody ready?" says the woman at the back of the motor boat pulling us. She's the safety surveyor, which seems completely unnecessary to me. "Hold on tight."

The banana boat launches forward and a blast of water hits me and my dad in the face. We chose the front for a more thrilling experience, but we had no idea what kind of thrill we were in for. The big rubbery boat rides the waves pretty smoothly at first.

"Not so bad!" dad says and rocks the front of the boat from side to side. The motor boat picks up speed and turns viciously to the left. The yellow boat leans deep into the centripetal force.

"Christ!" my mom shouts from the back.

The waves from the back of the motor boat begin to collide with the front of the flimsy banana we're straddling and we all pop up like rag dolls.

Dad's not bored anymore.

Up and down we flop with no control on the rubber boat and bounce off higher and higher with each wave. Our only chance of staying on the ride is to keep a death grip on the handles – the rest of our body is free to jump around with no control. The waves increase in frequency and height as the motor boat makes a right turn now.

"My arms! I'm gonna fly off!" I yell.

Dad's shouting about his bad knee in between propulsions into the air and mom's just barely hanging on in the back. I turn around to make sure she's OK.

"Hey mom, how ya doing back –" but I can't finish the sentence because the sight is too much to bear. Out. Of. Control. That's exactly what she is at that moment. Her body is flopping all over the surface of the rubber boat with her face down and her hair flying wildly in the wind, but miraculously her hands are still holding onto the boat. My arms grow weak from laughter. There is no dignity on the banana boat. My grip loosens with the image of mom plopping around in my mind and then before I know it, I am flying through the air and splashing into the ocean.

Thank god for my life jacket because the giddy feeling in my stomach has not passed. I am a bobbing hysterical buoy, feeling around for the bottom of my bikini before the boat circles back to get me.

How my mom managed to hang on I do not know.

They pull me back on the boat halfway and quietly watch me hoist myself up the rest of the way. I later realized they watched quietly because my bathing suit top had moved at some point in all the commotion and left the top half of my body inappropriately exposed. No shame on the banana boat. No shame.

The waterslides and free pina coladas are great, but it was the excitement of the banana boat ride that stays with us the longest. I can feel the strain of excitement in my arms for the rest of the day.

Our Last Night

We spend our last night in Aruba at our hotel's linen-cloth restaurant on the beach. My family and I like to pretend sometimes that we are sophisticated people who can go to places with this much class and refrain from making a scene, but our grace only lasts so long. During the first course, I notice that a crab has made its way up my dad's leg and onto his shirt.

"Hey dad, you've got a crab on your chest."

"What?" He scrambles in his chair and brushes off his shirt frantically, almost spilling the bottle of wine. The interruption is aggressive but brief. He pulls his chair back to the table as if nothing had happened, but us women can't let him get away with anything. My sister and mom take turns imitating his fleeting moment of terror while he grumbles, pretending to be mad.

I smile.

There's a warm evening breeze and a bittersweet taste in the air that's taking my mind away from my family's cheery state. 'This is our last night here,' I say to myself. 'Seven whole days of paradise and I feel like I've only just gotten here.'

A desperation takes over me: I didn't go in the water enough. I didn't walk on the beach as much as I should have. I shouldn't have left that wooden parrot souvenir – that would have been really nice to bring home. Regrets. Regrets. My cold's finally gone! It's gone and now we're leaving. I need one more day here, just one more night to –

"Hey, you OK?"

I've been picking at my fingernails. My sister knows I do this when I'm anxious.

Mom rubs my shoulder. "Sad about leaving, hon?" she asks.

"Yeah," I say, "real sad. I'm going to miss all the times like this."

"What? You mean your father making a fool out of himself? I'm sure they'll be plenty more times like this in the future." She smiles at dad and pinches him on the arm. "But seriously, don't worry. We have a lot to look forward to at home. The fun never stops."

Dad makes a gung ho gesture with his arm. "Yeah, we're a fun-filled family!"

"Oh god," my sister and I say together.

I watch a couple at a table a few feet away from us. They look about thirty years old - I can tell by the slight wrinkle at the edge of the woman's eye, softly glowing in the candle light. For a moment, I wish I were her, holding hands secretly behind the table's white cloth curtain with a man I love instead of my silly family. They are romantic and grown-up in every way, sipping red wine and gently talking rather making scenes or going straight for the bread basket like animals. The woman is dressed delicately in a blouse and they both have their elbows by their sides rather than on the table. After the waitress takes their order, I watch the man turn his body to face his sweet lover and meet her halfway for a kiss. Romantic and beautiful – just like the island. I wonder if I'll come here with a boy in the future. If I do, I probably won't look as serene as this couple. The genes I have inherited from my parents have cursed me to forever be an awkward, goof prone to problems such as unexpected colds, crab attacks, and banana boat accidents.

The couple separates from their kiss slowly and in unison, turn to look at me. Oops. And now I've ruined their tender moment. I quickly look down at my plate and chuckle to myself. Doomed. I am doomed.

I reenter my family and try to find my place in their conversation. Their chatter has taken a turn for the bizarre. My sister's discussing how horrifying it would be if one of us were digging our toes in the sand and suddenly felt a nose or some other facial feature in the ground and realized that there was a person buried under our dinner table. I call her creepy, and yet I continue the idea, thinking up strange scenarios, like if the person were alive and bit one of our toes to get our attention.

"Or wouldn't it be funny if the guy was just a weirdo and buried himself just so he could pop up every once and a while to say 'Hey!' and scare the heck out of tourists on the beach?"

The conversation progresses from a buried body to crazy people to the difference between actual crazy people and people who just act crazy to the difference between sorbet and sherbert to people who claim to hate chocolate when in truth, they are just liars.

"Have you ever tried pure chocolate though? It tastes like chalk. Maybe those chocolate-haters tried raw chocolate by mistake and are just confused."

"Who discovered that adding sugar and milk to chocolate would make it taste good anyway? Or even weirder, cheese. Who was the first person to try moldy, clumpy milk, or whatever it is, and convince other people to try it too?"

Dad paid the check a while ago, but we're all so enwrapped in our family debates about food and the important things in life that we stay till the kitchen closes. The couple at the table next to us left immediately after they paid their tab. I snuck a few more glances at them in between my family's ranting and raving and to be honest, they were pretty boring. They kissed more than they talked, which I suppose is sweet, but I realized that the serious, romantic scene just isn't me. I'll be here later in life with a great man I'm sure, but we'll be laughing and talking about stuff like this. We'll be affectionate and kiss too, but not to fill the spaces where fun and excitement are lacking.

I cringe to say this, but I love my family and I hope I stay just as awkward and funny as they are. Back home in Connecticut, the weather will be cold and awful compared to the heavenly days in Aruba, but at least I'll have my foolish crew traveling back home with me. This vacation, like so many of our other family vacations, is memorable not so much because of the scenery but because of the situations we wind up in and the wonderfully deranged ideas that pop into our heads and all those ridiculous little tiffs that turn into funny anecdotes to share later with my friends. My dad frequently tells me (in so many words) that it's not the setting that matters, but the person you are and the company you keep.

And damn it … that corny man is right.

By Melissa Toni

Vision

Walking alone I hear the creaking of trees moving in the wind. I look up to see the moody clouds as each foot fall brings me that much closer to what feels like the roof of the world. In the quiet I can hear the rumbling in the distance and I wonder if this is what the gods must know to be a lifetime or one single moment. This moment seems to stretch on forever and it could be possible to go backwards simply by turning around and walking the other way. The silence surrounding me turns the volume of my thoughts louder and my focus is settled into the comforting rhythms of footfalls as I crunch closer towards the frozen sky. Like so much of my life I wonder if I should stay invisible or if I should show myself to be more than a simple man. If I hear voices in the distance I wonder if I must come closer to the group or can I take the wilds of this air and wrap it into me by joining it with my own inner silence? At every shelter there are logs that people will pour their heart and soul into but I started out glancing at the first register in Georgia and found someone writing their life history. I imagine a scene from Kung Fu where the main character walks across the desert with a simple bag and plenty of flash backs. All the while he leaves little trace accept his footfalls and what he shares with those who listen. Walking in the world I pace through my memories under a brooding sky and begin to get closer to the idea of those I love. I have wanted to forget about the world and I never thought about isolation as a sensation until I understood the world to be left completely behind me.

To be seen in a crowd of four or five walking side by side seemed like a large family and at times overwhelming. Inside I grew quietly through the expression and dreams I was able to share with those around me. Yet my quiet took me to a place where I became part of the wind and I moved like water and my ideas could be just as formless. I invited the spirit of the wind to keep me company as I walked. It played with my hair and in the most silent of moments it made me feel like I was never alone. I could hear the leather of my jacket creak as I rested and I thought of the creaking forest moving just enough to say. "We recognize you here." I have walked through cracked and parched earth, beyond frozen mountain tops, and through the portals of my own brooding and musing ideas I sought to seek the edges of the earth so I might know the monsters and muses there and see myself as one of them. When I reached the end of that journey, I had a few pictures that now appear to be lost to time and I must have set them down in the same place where I allowed to settle the names of all those places I had been. I could not leave behind the connected knowledge of those places so I asked the wind to come with me.

Even today as I sit in a room and there are things dangling from the ceiling I play with the wind and I watch ceiling danglers turn in what appears to be the absence of wind. I am reminded of the trees swaying and the comfort of the world as I feel the swirling urge for open spaces by our elemental play. How easy it was to forget that comfort rarely lasted when temperatures dropped and the winds seemed like they would lift me high as a kite. Yet this seemed like just another barrier that signaled the crossing from world to world. There were times that the high canopies of trees rarely brook into full sunlight, which transitioned into ferns like I remembered the rain forests, waterfalls surprised my senses by prolonged anticipatory approaches, and flowers that I could not name greeted me. What I did not expect were moments that the landscaped was stripped, cut, and so baron it felt raped by pains mean made to make profit. When setting down to rest on a piece of packed snow the familiar tug of winds I learned can grow by gusts as if someone open up a tap. It is an odd sensation to feel your body being slid across the snow. My mind flashed to Carlos Castaneda and as if a Yaqui shaman had told me directly to grasp upon an object and shield me eyes until I could jump onto the back of a natural spirit I waited for the right moment.

It seemed I walked through a white out into a stinging wet blankness before those that I followed set down their lantern to pound the first peg into a frozen world. The winds changed and my thoughts followed it as I found it seemed awkward to think in words. I was not a practiced nagual holding my position along the mounting peaks of Mt. Katahdin. At any moment I might be lost or I may return to focus on those things left behind, those things enduring, and those things I have been fated to challenge. All things are present within this steady moment. It is only those things that are recognized that have the potential for me to notice them growing louder in the peripherals of my attention. In isolation I have recognized the distance inside that is without the tether of socialization. All the while I am coming back to the thought if I wish to be invisible on this twisting and even if I did I have to wonder how it is that I have been known. How it is that I have been seen. As I put this away I reflect back to that moment I thought it was too much trouble to wait for that stranger to leave his mark on the AT register. Even as I am about to walk across the US boundary at Mount Katahdin's Baxter Peak a part of me has regretted that I will finish this trail entirely invisible to the records. Yet the person who started this somehow is not the one who has penned these lines... I regret not being able to look back on his words and thoughts. It is the man that I am now that will further the dreams of wild beasts and impish men by the myths of striving to continue the passion and adventure of living. At the moment my eyes cannot get past an idea of a warm bed and the hands in which I will place mine..

By Joseph A. Santiago

Photography by Jillian Chase

Middle America

Two For the Price of One

Essays
Musings
Memoirs
and

.Everything Else.

A Mayan Experience: A URI Physical Therapy Student Service-Learning Project in Guatemala

This story is written with hope that it reflects the professional and personal benefits and challenges of student participation in volunteer work in a developing nation.

In December 2005, 5 students and I traveled to San Juan la Laguna, Guatemala for two weeks to provide physical therapy services in a center for children with disabilities. I hoped that the trip would provide an opportunity for the students to learn through experiences that were meaningful and by solving problems in real-life situations. Because I believe that learning through service is a way for students to experience and apply their knowledge, and that exposure to a diverse setting and culture facilitates broad and flexible thinking in terms of clinical and personal experience, I felt that the trip would benefit them at personal, interpersonal, community, and global levels. Ultimately, I hoped that the students would have an opportunity to practice their therapy skills on real people, stretch their clinical comfort zone, develop as clinicians, grow as people, and expand their world view.

The Journey

Early on a very cold December morning we meet at the airport and gathered together with our luggage. There is a palpable sense of nervous anticipation mixed with the early morning fatigue that follows a night of fitful sleep. We double check to be sure everyone has their travel documents. Then we laugh and get in line with all of the things we are bringing; a wheelchair, a large therapy mat wrapped in black garbage bags and duct tape, our extra bags containing bubbles, stickers, hair elastics and coloring books, and several power tools. The security agents have a field day.

I have made the trip once before, but my five student companions (Mark, Shannon, Jess, Amy, and Alicia) have never been to Guatemala. Three of the students have never left the United States! I am filled with excitement for them and for what they are about to see and experience.

Hurricane Stan, just two months earlier, nearly put an end to our trip. The mudslides washed out major roads, and killed hundreds of people in mountainside villages surrounding Lake Atitlan where we are headed.

During the last hour of the flight, it is difficult to take your eyes from the spectacular mountain ranges below. A rough landing in Guatemala City finishes a restful and uneventful flight. Dazed but excited, we enter the stifling airport. Jess and Amy use the bathroom and notice the first of many "Do not put toilet paper in the toilet!" signs. It doesn't take long to get accustomed to the new practice of putting used toilet paper into the trashcan, but every once in a while on the trip someone reports - with embarrassment - that they forgot and returned to their old ways. It is inevitable that this prompts a similar confession from someone else.

We wait nearly an hour and a half for the final pieces of our luggage to be spit out onto the squeaky, slowly moving, luggage belt. We take turns between manning the luggage belt and sitting with, and keeping count of, the bags that we have already retrieved. Over the next two days everyone comes to know the exact number and owner of the bags. Once we make arrangements to hire a van, we attempt to get ourselves through the throng of many hundreds of people just outside the doors of the airport. Each of us has our overstuffed backpack strapped on, and clings tightly to the other things we carry. Alicia looks like she might cry; the rest of the group giggles with concern at the confusion that surrounds us. Once in the van that takes us on to our next stop, we each take a deep breath, Amy counts the group members out loud and Mark does a quick accounting of our luggage. The ride to our hotel in Antigua is pretty quiet. Each of us watches out the windows in amazement as the noisy, congested, and exhaust-filled city gives way to lush, green, curvy mountainous roads. We marvel at ancient school busses, now customized with bright paints and dubbed "chicken" busses, filled to overflowing with riders and topped precariously with everything from bundles of avocados to baskets of, yes, chickens. Each time a "chicken" bus stops to pack in yet another passenger from the side of the road, a huge cloud of exhaust envelops our vanEveryone is wondering what we are in for over the next two weeks.

By American standards, Antigua seems primitive, but it is a beautiful city with crumbling, earthquake shaken architecture, tall walls that keep secret the gardens and homes behind them, and cobbled streets where tourists and natives walk in Western and traditional clothes. The few old cars, busses, and cabs rattle over the bumpy roads sending up dust in their wake. The streets in the center of town are lined with shops, Spanish emersion schools, small travel agencies, and restaurants. On our overnight stop we nap, explore, and celebrate our journey so far.

The next morning our driver, Joseo, in three hours, brings us from the civilization of Antigua - and other small dusty, polluted, and less attractive cities - over the cool mountains to Lake Atitlan. He drops us off at the makeshift dock that has been built to replace the one washed away by mudslides during the hurricane. A boat carries us across the deep lake surrounded by four volcanoes, from the dock in Panajachel to the south dock in San Pedro. We soak up the sun and get splashed as water comes over the low gunnels of the boat. The view is magnificent!!

At the rickety southern dock we disembark and three boys offer to help carry our bags along a dirt path through a corn field to our hotel. The boys are so small that they nearly buckle under the weight of some of the bags. Some of us take pictures of the boys with our great big backpacks on. We pay them a small amount, they leave happy. At the hotel sleeping arrangements are chosen and we settle into our very basic accommodations. Alicia checks for running water, which she reports is "only cold water." I speak to the manager about the water and I am told that he just needs to ignite the water heaters behind each room. We are dying for showers, but decide to wait and see if the hot water problem can be resolved. After making our rooms "our own" we inquire about the hammocks in front of some of the rooms. For about 50 cents a day we rent them and they become part of our end-of-the-day ritual;

a place where we relax and talk. The hammocks are also handy for stringing up hand-washed laundry to dry.

Everyone is anxious to explore the small town of San Pedro that will be "home" for the next two weeks. The town is built on a steep peninsula that juts into the lake. At the top of the hill is the town square and most of the locals' homes and shops. At the bottom of the hill, on either side of the peninsula, are the docks that are used by locals and tourists for transportation, delivery of goods, bathing, and fishing. The "Main Path" is a dirt foot path that winds along the bottom of the hill between the two docks. The path is the primary thoroughfare for locals and tourists connecting the small hotels, restaurants, and tiny shops. By the end of the trip the route is familiar and the people who work along, or frequent, the path become acquaintances. We come to learn their names, and they come to know ours. Mark is even given a special name in Tz'utujil, the local Mayan dialect.

Work at the Center

The short trip to the Centro Maya, in San Juan where we work each day, is a little adventure in itself. We get there in the same way that everyone gets around, on the back of a "pick-up." As many people as can possibly fit, cram into the small truck and stand holding onto the metal frame that transforms the tiny truck into a mass transit vehicle. We get artful at managing all of the things that we carry on the truck each day. The ride is exhilarating. Jess and Alicia put on their sunglasses to keep the bugs out of their eyes and when we get off the truck Jess asks whoever is closest to check her lip gloss for any small insects that might have gotten stuck. The only vehicles on the road are the "pick-ups" and the occasional "chicken" bus. Once in San Juan we walk down the steep hill to the center. People come out onto their stoops to say hello and watch us curiously as we pass. The students respond to children who practice their limited English vocabulary on us.

Shannon comments that the shock of the first day at the Center seems silly by the end of the trip. But when we arrive on the first day trepidation mixed with skepticism is evident in the students' faces. The three feet of mud that invaded the Center during "Stan" has been cleaned away and the structure is just as it had been previously: a long cinderblock building with five small separate rooms, a large outer classroom with a corrugated metal roof, an outdoor communal eating area, an outdoor sink area, a room with a toilet and spigot, and a small dirt yard with one small tree and lots of useless, old, rusting equipment. The cinder block building houses an office, a storage room, a therapy room, a small classroom, and a kitchen with a work table, a small refrigerator, and a Colman camping stove. A cinderblock wall topped with barbed wire surrounds the building.

The Center is full to capacity every day with the four Center staff members, volunteers from all over the world, and children. The center is for children with disabilities to be taught and get therapy, but because the local public school is out for the coffee harvest and Christmas break, there are many children who are there just for a meal and companionship. The youngest children are accompanied for the day by their mothers or older siblings. The Center is fun; it bustles with energy and activity. There is also a lot of work to be done. The only regular physical therapist comes once a week from Guatemala City. Because word has gone out that we were coming, there are many children to see for therapy. There are also several children to see in their homes in San Juan and other nearby villages.

Fabiola comes to the Center every day. She is a shy, sweet, 14 year old girl with cerebral palsy. She avoids us because she doesn't want to get her right arm and foot stretched. She would rather just hold hands. But with some playful teasing Amy gets her to submit to therapy.

Anna is a big, floppy girl who has the same pigtails in her hair all week. By Friday they are mass of snarls. She doesn't speak and smiles constantly. Anna doesn't need physical therapy, but she loves being bounced on the large, red therapy ball, so Jess indulges her from time to time. How can she resist?

Laura is an 18 year old girl who seems much younger. She seeks us out and seems to love the attention and conversation with us. Her intense gazes and winsome expressions make you want to help her somehow. Even with her missing front tooth, her smile is heartwarming.

Maria is 3 years old and a little difficult to look at. She is not cute. Shannon works with her on an old hospital bed that has no mattress. A blanket is spread over the springs to make it a little more comfortable. Maria requires daily stretching. All of her joints are severely deformed, especially her hands and feet. She cries constantly and frequently has to be nursed by her mother in order to calm down.

Melissa cries a lot too; especially when Shannon tries to work with her. A day or two into our visit she gets more comfortable and doesn't cry as much. She is a beautiful 2 year old who is not walking well. Her mother smiles and watches everything we do. Melissa's shoes are much too big and we feel that this is making it even harder for her to walk. We buy her some new shoes and they seem to help.

The poorest of the children come on a bus from San Pablo every day. Domingo is one of them. He is a 10 year old boy who has some sort of muscular dystrophy. He has a nice wheelchair that was donated to him last year. He hates to wear his seatbelt. This makes us very nervous since the surface conditions everywhere are treacherous for someone in a wheelchair. He needs therapy every day and smiles while Jess stretches his badly contracted legs and makes him exercise his weak shoulders. He is always filthy, but his huge smile and mischievous personality make you forget about that. He hides pipe cleaners, scissors, bits of string, and other little goodies under his legs to sneak them home. We ignore this.

Francisco and Flavio look so much alike that we often confuse them. Both are about 4 years old and both are silent. But, they are really very different. Francisco is deaf and blind. He can move quite a bit when he is out of his wheelchair. Jess helps him walk and do exercises. The wheelchair we brought with us is for Flavio. He is the youngest of eight children. Before he got the wheelchair his mother carried him everywhere on her back swaddled in a woven shawl. He has a severe seizure disorder which has rendered him completely passive. While Amy works with him he frequently has little seizures. Initially this worries her but after talking with his mother she is less concerned. He moves very little on his own and is at about a three month level of development. Flavio and Francisco are treated every day and the students show their mothers and the volunteers some activities and exercises to do after we leave.

Marta Ophelia is a big, twenty year old girl whose elderly mother and father take turns bringing her to the Center. They dote over her and frequently straighten her traditional clothing and wipe the drool from her chin. They say prayers for Mark and Shannon as they work with their daughter. It takes three people to lower her to the therapy mat on the floor and two people to carry out her exercises. Her wheelchair is literally falling apart. Mark and Shannon try to talk about getting her a new one, but for some reason – which they can't understand – her parents don't want a new one.

There are several adorable preteen girls who don't get physical therapy, but they huddle together and whisper as they listen to us and watch what Amy and Jess are doing. Victor, Ernesto, Juan, Ricardo, Romeo provide entertainment. Victor is 5. It looks like he has cut his own hair. He loves to ham it up and have his picture taken. Ernesto is 3. He is always running and jumping on people or speeding by on a lopsided tricycle. Juan, who is 10, is the Director's son. He has a deformed ear and very deformed hands. He likes to play catch and ride bikes. His hands don't seem to limit him at all. Ricardo is about 17 and has Down Syndrome. He has an adorable giggle and sits with Jess and Alicia as they make adjustments to braces and sew curtains to keep the hot sun out of the new outdoor treatment room that is being built. Ricardo wears the Red Sox hat that Mark gave him, and likes to borrow Jess' sunglasses. Romeo must have been a politician in another life. He welcomes us every morning like he has never met us before. He has the same conversation each day. He has a loud voice and an infectious laugh. From time to time he answers the broken cell phone in his pocket with a loud "Hola."

Home Visits

Each day some of us leave the center and visit children in their homes. Alicia and Jess walk back up the steep hill into the center of San Juan and follow confusing directions that lead down dirt roads and along winding footpaths between houses built so close together that only one at a time can pass. "The Juans" – two brothers, both named Juan – live in a very typical house. A large hinged metal door encloses the compound which is made up of a small cinderblock building for sleeping, an outdoor kitchen with an open fire, a family area covered with corrugated metal, an outhouse, and a garden area. Chickens wander in and around then back into the corn stalks that grow right next to the house. The Juans' mother and sister make tamales for the Festival of Mary. Younger siblings play with a new puppy, "Balto". Sometimes the father is there and watches what we do. Juan and Juan are ten years apart in age, but both of them stopped growing when they were about five. One of the Juans has a twin sister who was spared from whatever their strange disease is, and is now a beautiful 18 year old woman. Alicia and Jess work with them on a straw mat that is put down on the cement floor. It is easy to pick them up and move them, but both Juans just barely tolerate the therapy of stretching and moving. When Alicia and Jess leave the family members repeatedly expresses their appreciation and thanks.

Despite our repeated efforts, Rosalia's mother won't let us treat her. Rosalia is 16 and is severely disabled by cerebral palsey. Both of her legs sweep off to the right and her arms are held bent and tightly against her sides. Flies linger around her constantly wide open mouth. Her mother's understanding of why Rosalia might need physical therapy seems to be limited. We design and build an adapted chair that will get Rosalia up off of the dirt floor, and maybe reduce the huge callus on her left hip. On our last day we put the chair over the fence and into her yard, hoping that her mother will give it a try.

Manuel is a bright 12 year old boy who goes to the public school. One of the Center volunteers asks Amy and me to visit him to see what ideas we have about him using a computer. When we arrive at his house he and his brother are sitting on the spotlessly clean, painted cement floor playing cards. Manuel holds his cards between his toes. He does everything with his feet even though his leg function is minimal. His arms are non-functional. Not only are his limbs of very little use, they are fixed in disruptive positions, and make it difficult for him to fit into the wheelchair he has. Neither of us has ever seen anyone like Manuel and we marvel at what he is able to do with such significant disability. With the volunteer, we discuss various equipment options that might help him use a computer. A computer would make a world of difference for this child, and we hope someone follows through with getting one for him.

Each of us is especially touched by Jesus, a 9 year old boy who lost his home in Hurricane Stan just two months before our visit. He and his family live in a temporary house which they have to move out of soon. Jesus contracted Guillian-Barre after the storm, and he is just beginning to regain some function after being paralyzed by the disease. Shannon mentions that she hopes he is one of the many who regain full function as the disease resolves. On our first day his father carries him to the center on his back. Because he must work, and can't get Jesus to the Center every day, so we agree to go to the house to treat him. In the dusty yard of the house, Amy and Mark show him exercises on a foam rubber mat with tattered edges. They also have him try to walk in a set of makeshift parallel bars that his father has constructed from sticks. The whole family, including his grandmother, is devoted to Jesus, and participates in some way with his therapy. His grandmother frequently cries as she laments Jesus' condition and worries about his fate and the fate of the family. Amy cries too and says she is worried about the same things.

The Community and the Culture

When we're not at the Center we are busy soaking up all that we can about the community and the culture. The students are desperate to make use of every bit of time that they have. Just walking in town is an adventure. Stray dogs, a major problem in San Pedro and San Juan, wander the "Main Path", follow us home, and join us at dinner in restaurants. We plan our trip to the "pick-ups" each day so that we get to walk through the market at the center of town. We soak in the confusion, smells, noises, and sights. The Catholic Church in the main square is always busy and we watch people coming and going in traditional dress and carrying Bibles. The coffee harvest is underway and we try to learn about it by watching and asking questions of the men working at the small street-side coffee processing plants.

It doesn't take long for us to notice that besides the children that are nervous when we try to work with them at the Center, we never see a child crying. The children are kind to each other, content and happy. Children of all ages walk hand-in-hand down the street. It is common to see five or six year old children caring for their younger siblings. They do not have many toys, but they are able to play with and make fun out of any available thing. Children help their parents with major household chores without complaint.

On our fourth night in San Pedro we're told that we should go to the main square for a festival that night. None of us has ever experienced anything like the Festival of the Ascension of Mary. The fireworks are sporadic early in the day and become more regular as the day goes on. It is dark when we arrive but there is an incredible crescent moon overhead. We wander the square listening to bands playing traditional music and watching children set off small firecrackers. We are all energized and wait excitedly to see what unfolds. Everyone in San Pedro is there. At about nine o'clock hundreds of fireworks explode and Mary emerges from the front of the church. Thirty women, with their heads draped in matching shawls, walk slowly and reverently carrying the platform where Mary stands on their shoulders. The beautiful statue of Mary is dressed in traditional Mayan clothing and draped in a shawl similar to those that the women carrying her wear. Her platform is elaborately decorated with flowers and lights. In addition to those carrying her, a massive crowd of women surrounds and follows Mary. Several men follow behind with a small generator that powers the lights. Mary spends the next three hours circling the village with continuous fireworks leading her way. The noise is incredible and from time to time we have to cover our ears. We wonder when they will let up - but they don't. We take a break from the deafening noise by ducking in to a small restaurant for a hot chocolate. We sit for a while then decide we should try to get a good spot for Mary's return and the grand finale. The street is now covered with pine needles and lined with long lengths of small firecrackers. Mary approaches the main square, and the elders, who are in charge of the fireworks, set up canisters from which they will shoot huge, home-made explosives. We watch in amazement and fear and reconsider where we have chosen to stand. This is when the real frenzy starts. We decide that maybe we should move back a little from the fireworks that are littering down debris. We are surrounded by the crowd and have to boost ourselves over a tall wall to gain distance from the explosions. We are completely caught up in what is going on. Shannon admits that she is a little afraid but doesn't want to miss anything. The finale, as Mary reenters the church, is a beyond description crescendo of music, fireworks and cheering. We, somehow, have managed to stay together. We hold on to each other and weave our way out of the crowd and down the hill toward our hotel. The Festival of Mary will not soon be forgotten.

Local People

In just our short time in San Pedro we become acquainted with many local people. On our first day we meet Yolanda and Magdalena. By the second day they know each of us by name. Yolanda and Juanita work as a pair selling fresh-baked bread on the street. Yolanda's right eye is cloudy and she tells us that selling bread is helping her to make money to pay for cataract surgery. They find us every day and expect us to buy bread. On most days we do, but on the days that we don't, we get looks of disappointment and reprimand. By the end of our time in San Pedro we try to avoid them.

In the late afternoons, Amy, Jess and Alicia take weaving lessons from Angela at her home. They sit on cinderblocks and learn to weave using traditional hand-constructed looms that span from the weaver's waist to the branches of an orange tree in the yard. It is hard, back-breaking work. While they are weaving they experience the life of the household around them. In between her other chores, Angela's daughter helps to correct their mistakes. The students bring small gifts for Angela's son. He gives them hugs each day when they arrive. Despite the language barrier, Angela and her family and the students come to know each other pretty well by the time their weaving projects are done. From then on, whenever they see a woman weaving the students comment on the difficulty and perfection of her work.

As part of an assignment that the students must complete, Angela offers to take us to meet her grandfather, Santos, and his wife, Magdalena. Amy, Jess, Alicia and I climb steep, narrow paths to the home where they live with about ten other family members of all ages. We are welcomed in to their home and Alicia and Jess use their somewhat limited Spanish to have a conversation with Santos and Magdalena about what it is like to be elderly in rural Guatemala. The students are moved by the "awesome" opportunity and realize what a special experience it is. Magdalena takes us to where she sells candy and chips on the side of the street, and we are introduced to her friend, Isabella, who takes us with her to where she has her corn ground into tortilla meal. Amy comments that she thinks we have had a priceless experience that most visitors to San Pedro don't get to have.

Mayra is an 11 year old girl who balances a basket of small bracelets, woven purses and key rings on her head. At night she walks from restaurant to restaurant selling the items in her basket to tourists. The money she makes helps to support her family. We meet her while having dinner on our second night. Mayra does not go to school but she is smart and has picked up some English from tourists. She makes herself comfortable and sits with us at the table. We offer to buy her a drink and she accepts. At one point she takes some nail polish out of her pocket and offers to paint my fingernails, which the students think is "adorable". After that, Mayra eats with us nearly every night. We send our leftovers home to her family. Her sense of humor and big dimples entertain us and lighten some of the fatigue we feel at the end of our busy days. Our friendship grows and Mayra meets us at our hotel to hang out with us when we get back from the Center in the evenings. She loves to brush Jess' long blonde hair. Some days she brings her younger siblings, Andrea, Mario, and Martita to hang out too. We give them lots of the little things that we have brought; stickers, bubbles, candy, hair ties, toothbrushes, markers and other things. They are so excited and thankful for every item. One night at dinner Amy is talking with Mayra about Christmas. During the conversation she tells Amy that her family does not have the money for any decorations. On our way through the market Amy suggests that we buy some Christmas decorations and decorate Mayra's house. We do and then Amy, Jess and I make our way to Mayra's. Her mother is there and greets us with kisses of welcome and gratitude for our friendship with Mayra. Their house is shockingly small. The children proudly show us around the outside kitchen area and the one room where all six family members live. The room contains nothing more than two double beds and a bureau. Their belongings are piled along the perimeter of the room. We string up the sparkly garlands in and around the house and hang ornaments from the lemon tree in the front yard. The whole family seems delighted. We are completely choked-up and at a loss for words. We hug them good-bye and wish them "Feliz Navidad". Amy, Jess and I wordlessly hug each other as we head down the hill and back to the hotel. When we tell the rest of the group, they immediately understand what a powerful experience it had been.

On the Weekend

On the weekend, when the Center is closed, we have time for some rest and opportunity to explore the region a little more. We all have some Christmas shopping to do so on Saturday we head across the lake to the large market in

Panajachel. We spend several hours buying drums, hand woven and embroidered textiles, machetes, jade earrings, small Mayan figurines, brightly painted masks, t-shirts and other gifts to bring home. We are often surrounded by people trying to sell us various things and we hold on tight to the fanny packs that contain our money. Alicia, in particular, gets very good at bargaining for the lowest price on things. Mark expresses his frustration at trying to translate the language and the money into something that makes sense. When we get to the point where we can't carry anything else, we head back to the dock for the boat ride home.

Angela, the weaving instructor, helps us arrange a guide for a hike up to "La Narez", the "nose" of the profile shaped mountain ridge that looms over San Juan. We are met by Moses, our guide, at 4:30 on Sunday morning. We have a 45 minute ride in the back of a pick-up truck through the pitch black morning to the ascending trailhead. Once there, we hike up for about another 45 minutes. Moses has timed it perfectly so that we are at the peak just in time for the sunrise. We are so excited to be there and the view is breathtaking. Mark comments that he can't believe he even thought twice about whether or not to get up so early. Pictures are taken of the view and of ourselves with Moses and his machete. For about an hour we talk and eat our breakfast. Then Moses says we should begin our four-hour descent so that we're down before it gets really hot. The hike down is beautiful, but steep and a little treacherous in parts. At the end of the hike we are all proud of each other and have experienced a special bond. Back in San Pedro, after we shower off the thick dust that coats our bodies, we treat ourselves to a relaxing lunch.

Day-to-Day

During the whole trip communication is difficult. We don't have nearly enough Spanish, and certainly even less Mayan. Jess says she gets a headache just trying so hard to listen, understand, and get a point across. It's a little embarrassing at first but soon we get accustomed to looking and sounding silly using a combination of broken Spanish, broken English, and the local Mayan dialect, along with hand gestures, facial expressions and demonstrations to communicate with all of the people we interact with. The students say that, amazingly, this type of communication generally does the trick. Alicia who has the most Spanish, says that she is frustrated because she knows she is missing details, specifics and subtleties. But we realize how rich our communication has been even without perfect understanding.

Meals are important. Breakfast each day is a time when we energize, gear-up and plan for the day ahead. The coffee is great. Lunch is more haphazard and we are often in several different places so we eat granola bars or street food. Most of the time, all of us eat dinner together. Mayra joins us until about eight thirty when she has to go home. There are excellent restaurants and meals are leisurely and delicious. The weather allows us to eat outside almost every evening. One restaurant shows a movie on a big screen after the dinner rush. At another, we sit at a table next to an open fire pit. Dinner is a time when we relax, laugh, and tell stories of our daily adventures. We debrief and come together as a tight-knit group. On our last night in San Pedro, Jess expresses that the dinner is joyous and sad at the same time.

At the end of each day we spend a little time lying in our hammocks or on a spot on the ground, enjoying the incredibly clear sky. Because there is no ambient light, the moon and stars are clearer than we've ever seen. We try, rather pathetically, to identify constellations. We count falling stars for a while and then, one-by-one, excuse ourselves for bed. We sleep well after being lulled by the sound of the waves on the lake.

The Way Home

After our last trip back across Lake Atitlan, as previously arranged, Joseo is there to pick us up. Because the main road is blocked by protestors, he says we have no choice but to take the more mountainous and circuitous route. We settle in for a long, bumpy, and sometimes precarious, drive along roads where the areas that had been washed out in the hurricane are still evident - and in some places nearly impassable. It is beautiful, but several people comment that they can't wait to get to our hotel in Antigua where a hot shower with good water pressure and a comfortable bed awaits us.

Antigua seems familiar and civilized when we return. We spend the day we have there sightseeing and doing some last minute shopping. We have a celebratory final dinner together. The excitement of getting home is hitting all of us and we begin to transition back into our non-San Pedro selves. We talk less about our experiences and more about the final leg of our trip.

Before we know it we are saying good-bye to each other in the airport and heading our separate ways. Out of habit we count to see if everyone has the appropriate number of bags. We make plans to get together soon for dinner and to share pictures. We have to get together soon. Because, we all realize that even with pictures, our families and friends at home won't be able to feel the same things that we feel about all of our stories and adventures.

Discussion

In the course of this experience, the students and I had the opportunity to practice our therapy skills on real people, stretch our clinical comfort zones, and develop as clinicians. We had to work creatively in very basic therapy settings, with limited resources and limited communication. We treated children who have severe, and often poorly attended to, disabilities. We had to be flexible and adjust to a variety of circumstances.

Each of us experienced personal growth and was immersed in a community and culture that expanded their world view. We met, worked with, interacted with, and in some cases, developed close relationships with several local people – young and old. Our communication skills were challenged and required creativity and flexibility. We had the opportunity to experience, first hand, cultural differences related to disability, work, money and lifestyle.

During the trip there was significant opportunity for discussion about the clinical and cultural experiences. This daily discussion and sharing optimized the overall experience. Strong bonds and friendships grew.

But, most importantly, each of the participants felt that the trip was "a life-changing experience" both professionally and personally. For many the trip had been a leap of faith. For some it was a risk-taking experience. For all it was an exciting adventure.

Since that first trip, I have taken many more students to the same place. Each trip leaves me in awe of the experience. Each group becomes like a family. Each group accomplishes amazing things. Each group has unique, wonderful, and sad experiences. Each person comes home changed forever.

Included below are some comments made in written reflections following the trip:

"I had many fears about the trip... In researching the country it did not seem like a place I wanted to go... (but) I would have regret(ed) not taking the chance. It really was like a "live life to the fullest", "live every day as if it were your last" type of thing for me. And in the end I was so grateful that I had decided to go because it did end up being one of the most amazing almost indescribable experiences of my life." (Alicia)

"As a personal experience, I'm still feeling the effects. I had never left the country, never gone on a true adventure." (Amy)

"... I am so glad that I went. It was the best experience I have had in so many different ways – it is so hard to explain." (Jess)

"... I will never (again) look at a child... or an ill-equipped clinic and think nothing can be done. It was amazing to see how much could be done with so little." (Amy)

"I feel this trip really helped me to become more confident in my therapy skills. I feel we kind of got thrown into the fire, and it was either sink or swim – I wouldn't have had it any other way... I feel I had to be a creative PT and work with what I had, and work through the communication barrier." (Jess)

"They welcomed us into their homes and were very willing to show us how they cook, live, and work. They take such pride in what they do and are so open to talk about themselves." (Alicia)

"I was lucky enough to have great experiences with the families... who offered nothing but love and support to their children, which was not what I had expected. But their unconditional love and acceptance for their child was

overwhelming and could be felt even through the language and cultural barriers." *(Amy)*

"Guatemalans always say "hello" or "good morning" whether they know you or not. It made you feel good and welcomed in the community." *(Jess)*

"Looking into the eyes of some of the children – especially the Juans who cannot speak, I felt sometimes that I just knew what they felt or what they were trying to say. A connect between people can be made at any level without speaking." *(Jess)*

"I can still remember each child, each person, each scene, each day- as if it were yesterday. I guess that's how you know you were affected, how your life has been changed. My life was definitely changed. I feel as if I not only learned a wealth of information for my physical therapy career, but for my personal life..." *(Amy)*

"One (of my most memorable experiences) is when we brought decorations to Mayra's family; the look on the children's faces and the tears in their mother's eyes because of a few dollars worth of Christmas decorations." *(Jess)*

"I learned a lot about myself during the two weeks: that I could make do with little, that I could travel on my own, that I could connect with people I didn't know and would never understand." *(Amy)*

"I miss hanging out with (everyone)! I had such an amazing time, it sometimes consumes me... I find myself looking through (the) photos everyday..." *(Mark)*

"Everyday I wish I had more, I remember the children who had nothing and were happy to be given a sticker or a hair tie." *(Amy)*

"The trip was amazing. I learned a lot about the Guatemalan culture and a lot about myself... I never thought I would ever say this, however, I look forward to taking another trip to Guatemala..." *(Alicia)*

"I miss (everyone) and can't imagine going with any other group. I feel so fortunate to have met and been able to spend so much "quality" time together. Although our time was limited in the grand scheme of things, I feel that we were able to make a difference in the people's lives and I think we all learned a lot about ourselves and what we are able to accomplish." (Shannon)

"There are so many things that I can't even express that impacted me on this trip. I am so glad to have had this experience because it really was life altering. It has definitely changed my views on many things and has made me a better person." (Jess)

"Being a part of such a thing was an extremely rewarding experience." (Alicia)

"The trip was fabulous and it is just too hard to explain (to people) though pictures do help." (Shannon)

"As much as PT was the focus of the trip, I feel that I learned so much more about myself. That was most important." (Jess)

"I feel truly blessed to have been given this amazing experience. This is a trip I could have never planned on my own, or ever have imagined by myself. I loved every minute of it: from the long trip there and back, to the hours on end of weaving classes, the language barriers, the kids, the truck rides, the food, the solar pools, the dogs, the friends, and all the memories." (Amy)

By Jennifer Audette

A Small Stone of Wonder

Sometimes at night I feel like my mind begins to hum like a spinning piece of machinery that cannot help but disturb its supposed operator. It seems that I give my mind a license to wander and daydream while asleep so that patterns might be organized and drawn together like the tightening strings of a girdle. And this pulled so tightly to design in rules that may become the foundation of wonder from which I may jump... In free fall from everyday thoughts I explore what is possible with only the limits of my current imaginings. Tomorrow's a choice that could be made to go one way instead of another because of sheer curiosity or desire to bring myself to something new.

Where does a sleepless mind go if not deeper into wonder when the world seems all silent and dreaming? Walking through castles in the sky, characters emanate from the indigenous wonderment to give my inner life voice. How one character is imbued with nobility and another with the feeling of uncertainty seems to be beyond the dreamer at first glance. Holding onto a world propped up by toy soldiers of desire, wishes, intent, and the remarkable bad banana before bed, all of the reflections and impressions tumble about and planning what comes next. There are times when the darkest of nights will be needed to bring to our attention the safe harbor so we seek by its light. Wonder is a matter of how I find myself in relationship to everything else.

Serious wonder propels me into a future where the territory of wonderment is taken seriously. A matter of development and experience, one instance becoming the vehicle of what I might handle next. The fuel of my thoughts becomes my excitement as I feel myself moving. My body is designed to move and my mind to discover a spirit relationally interpreted by that acts that are held worthy to wonder. As a tree holds itself up by its roots, I believe we are held by the inquisitive desire of life so we might explore its wonder. Sometimes I wonder if something that I may say to another person might be the last thing they ever hear, or the last thing that I ever get to say to them. Sometimes I forget the questions that move me as I watch the empty air support the weight of a bird...

All without words I move back and forth across that indivisible line of waking dreams to challenge sleeping consciousness in an attempt to understand unconscious wonder. The newness and awe that comes from beauty, experience, and accomplishments, sits at the peaks of understanding that I seek to reach. The tumbling of notions, events, and experiential dreams, will set my eyes to landscapes of wonder, but it will be up to me to question, stretch, and reach. I wonder if I look far more often inside myself then I do outside, and what if outside is but another inside? Each question is a journey and an invitation to open up a universe that leads me back into myself. Who then is this "I" that honestly wonders?

By Joseph A. Santiago

A Story of Un

Un embodies the shape of a capsule broken in half and containing a perspective of reference that is descriptive of the frame being nailed upon experience. When I think of what happened yesterday I imagine a movie of events playing just under eye level on my left and it replays in a wide screen rectangle as I think of it. Since this memory is already encapsulated within my memory I have subconsciously organized it into a frame in which there are two sides. I can imagine seeing myself paying attention to that memory as I walk around to look at it from the other side.

The perspective underneath everyday processing reveals to me many things about the way I am thinking about life, and thus how I relate to the ocean of variables and elements encountered before my first breath. The Un perspective brings a prescriptive quality to the "I" of an observer, so the descriptive awareness of being more than an idle participant can open up awareness even just a little bit more. The memory of what happened yesterday has rested seemingly solid, until touched like a still pool, showing it to be understandably responsive to the ripples of my thoughts and interaction. Any experience by itself, is capable of being restructured, because it is the unstable reflection of practiced perspective. The mirror of the mind following its well traced roots into form while seeking connection and depth of breadth between known and unknown. One aspect of universal continuity may indeed lead into the whole, but it's not until it's connected by thought that it will be known to be so.

Seeking more than a reaction to the undetermined reality that stands tall around my underlying thoughts I seek the levers to play in my sandbox. Looking out through my perspectives, I am always curious if what I will find is what I thought I'd seen as the whole picture. While it might take a lie to recognize the truth, I don't believe the slices of truth that each of us can be aware of is any more or any less than a fragment of unrealized opportunities of expression. Moving parallel through my thoughts into a position of an unabashed participatory investigation infuses the unrealized happenings of an event into a further exploration of identity.

The capsule that Un contains is the stories of life and is bent like light through a prism. The infinite unassuming universe is somehow squeezed and limited through the acceptance of ideas preaching an unambiguous singular expression and path expected to contain the unyielding expression that is me. I have found the strung pearls of opposites as an opportunity for growth and part of the undertow of change. Un is the unraveling of position and perspective so we might see ourselves as a living Universe pushing and pulling through the currents of change that extend far beyond the lines children might color in. I am moved unaware of the universal stories that extend beyond this undiscovered moment. I wander forward as a partially unknown perspective sharing my story of Un.

By Joseph A.Santiago

Emptiness is Not a Box

Emptiness is not a box and yet it holds everything close. The world is piled in over emptiness as if it were the soil for the world to grow. I imagine emptiness to be the dividing line between here and somewhere else. Holding onto the picture of a cardboard box so heavily taped together from the many times I have moved I begin to wonder... How many things have slipped from here to there, and from there to here once they knew how? Like a fish in water, I have forgotten that I bump and bother the ocean of air that sustains me. Perhaps emptiness is the ocean that floats all that we can see. It's invisible substance being the very thing that nourishes all the possibility that can be... Destiny. This is all done between the groaning spirals that might be games. Each move played through a snowballing universe that could contain the heavens.

Once in a while I look out at the vastness of space and see the colors of a sunset, a swaying field of grain, and the crashing of the waves. All the while asking myself how this reflects emptiness, and somehow the information is communicated from there to here. Somehow, all these little bits of something speak to me without words. My concept of what is opposite of here will always be there, but will the same cognitive point be shared amongst us for these undiscovered flip-flops. Silently embracing us and subtly whispering to us, emptiness seems to have a message that touches each of us in gentle ways.

As part of everything that we see and inside all that we know ourselves to be, I may be the first to question if I am one of emptiness's children. One of the animate universes that seeks to explore and venture into the game by the interactions of the restless vehicles of life. All of we children of emptiness holding onto the formless forms that keep us seeking to know the forms that we embody, imagine, adopt, and design through our unrelenting curiosity.

Every thought must be pregnant with the delight of emptiness and the next possibility. I must make sure then that my thoughts are good ones.

There may be no here or there for the children of emptiness. It seems to be all a matter of belief and perspective that can move me to once again seek out the experiences that communicate to me about my roots of emptiness.

By Joseph A. Santiago

Impossible to Return Home

Nostalgia powerfully grips (like a vise wound and coiled tight) upon the mind when mental and physical debility (and sometimes senility wrought by the ravages of age) force and oust departure from a residence chock a block full of memories! Assaults upon cognizant ability to function and perform daily tasks wreak havoc in the abstract and concrete edifices (built over a lifetime) and lay waste with indiscriminate and wanton destruction in a psychological maelstrom, which rents asunder all psychic strength formerly providing an ability to weather trials and tribulations encompassing the Homo Sapiens internal landscape. Components serving as ramparts to buttress integuments via carefully nourished defenses and cherished from countless (perchance infinite in scope)odds and ends, precious mementos, and personal belongings filling every nook and cranny within interstitial temporal lobe battered and weakened! In short, the domain to sustain and uphold willpower to beat back and fend off agents provocateurs (disguised as ineluctable and insidious degenerative denizens) renders to maintain a vibrant fight to live a more or less lost cause!

Such a scenario happens to be the case with Sylvia Zison, which major subject (and unsuspecting player) of this essay is also related to me by marriage. Her youngest daughter Abby happens to be my spouse of almost seven years, whose father (the late William Zison) inadvertently contributed (via departure from the living realm from a protracted combination of chronic afflictions) after fifty plus years of marriage, to wretched woes felt by his wife. Although not necessarily a sudden and unexpected death (whence corporeal being reclaimed by terra firma, which constituent molecules to be recycled), such cessation of existence (akin to last word of the final passage inscribed in our individually custom made book of life) represents end of mortality and segue way affianced into journey ascribed as the afterlife, the beyond, crossing over, heaven, the other side or paradise , to list just six terms when lack of breath (robbing one of the keen sport to let biscuits fly) determines a coroner to confirm that a mortician can prepare corpse for burial!

Death (despite such ordinary expectation and prediction) still issued grievous impact and even now (approaching the fourth anniversary of consciousness termination) undermines the capacity of aforementioned matriarch to escape and shake off the mantle of suffering from one of the most severe losses one can experience. This is currently witnessed by an entrenched, serious and tragic depression.

The next eldest sibling, Octavia Lamb (ten years separates the two siblings) resides in Gap, Pennsylvania. She occupies the title of principal caretaker (by dint of circumstance) of said mother in law, whose frail health and vulnerable emotional state (at nearly eighty years old) require constant attention and vigilance.

Plaintive pleas regularly voiced in barely audible and weak utterances to occupy her former demesne! Want to know the sad truth about the matter? Lack of necessary faculties prevent the freedom to leave the assisted living community, an arrangement representing perhaps an equally unhappy setting (which intermittent riffs) arise from cramped quarters and exorbitant cost and move back into said domicile, the dwelling at 1148 Greentree Lane, Narberth, Pennsylvania, 19072 currently housing kith (of this writer) hitherto identified as Harris clan.

Helplessness (on my part) touched me to the quick and prompted an attempt to build a compassionately conservative composition based on this theme stated as follows. Departure from safety and security of hearth imposed either by travails of gerontological processes or biological vibrancy witnessed on the opposite end of the chronological spectrum to be adopted as a metaphor per transformation from dependent grownup succumbing to childlike role or (visa versa) young person to become independent older individual. Profound and necessary heart wrenching bouts experienced when separation (either chosen out of free will or forced by decree) felt from harsh systemic erosion or autonomy against parental figures assail the psyche with paroxysms of so called homesickness! The latter aspect encompasses essence of my thesis. Proper growth and maturation of body, mind and spirit triage predicated on ability to get out from under the powerful and strong authoritarian domination (unavoidable even with a loving and supportive father and mother) and rely on the resources and skills inherent within the self.

Trials are most severe when freshly minted high school graduates shear the figurative and psychological umbilical cord via bold and drastically made decisions that challenge and expand parentally pronounced parameters. Invisible demarcation are like boundary markers foisting a geographical gulf. Outside that range, the fertile imagination conjures up images filled with dark, foreboding and sinister notions. Bridges (figurative and literal connecting an unknown future to a familiar past) are well nigh impossible to erect, and hence not available to access and traverse connections with father and mother in direct proportion to the number of miles away from home.

Once the onset of legitimately recognized adulthood is reached (a mere stripling of eighteen or twenty-one tender years depending on the State of residency) many females and males (in this post-adolescent stage) hanker to test their mettle and natural propensity to conduct life choices frequently in direct contra-distinction to their upbringing. Such phase of life governed in part by an innate predilection to explore the man-made and natural world awash in diversity, history (anthropological, cultural, geological, musical, philological, etc.), limitless poetic and prosaic inspiration, topological variety, etc., yet held in check if only temporarily toward maternal and paternal links.

Emancipation from role of legal (co)-dependant arrangement (enumerated in those coveted, enshrined and treasured documents along with additional codified declarations), not only guarantees acquisition of civil, fiscal, marital, political, reproductive, and statutory rights to mention only a half dozen, but full-fledged significant birth date attainment also allows, enables and provides realization to behold a sudden gamut of liberty and pursuit of happiness (without impingement and jeopardy to another citizen) to the extent of ambitious zeal. Hapless youths giddy with an intoxicating stupor (freighted with buoyant and vital passion) exercise a powerful penchant to unleash the pent up potential to plot personal paths.

Authentic license automatically possessed when specific requirements met spelled out and stipulated in sacred scriptures penned by founding fathers of these United States. One of these highly recognized critical items unacknowledged by signatories concerns privilege to drive and own a vehicle. Transportation remedies hidebound restraint and makes temptation very appealing to accede obeisance toward mobile wheels of fortune. Ventures to travel over hills and dales (afar off in the distance) beckons, calls and awakens the frontier element. A gentle and warm welcome dispenses treasures galore when surrendering the whim to traverse highways and nearly limitless vista beyond horizon!

Prospects abound to roam hither and yon (in a footloose and fancy free nomadic style) and decide how long to remain in an especially aesthetically alluring locale if the collegiate endeavor happens to be unfavorable or unsuitable. Whether drawn to concoct a vagabond (seat of pants some might label hair brained scheme) gallivanting and globe-trotting trekker mode (crisscrossing one continent after another), or prefer more discipline and structured academic tradition (with opportunity to partake trappings of campus life from an accredited college or university) while attempting to pursue a particular degree, the day of reckoning may dawn to revisit that formative abode.

As that day to enter the domicile replete with autobiography approaches (after satisfactory hiatus), a heightened awareness, measurable increase and palpable sensations of anxiety, apprehension, jittery nerves, panic attacks, uncertainty ratchets up quite a few notches and triggers spikes in adrenaline hormone and perforce additional physiological ramifications. This first reunion with kindred folks no doubt fraught with intense reaction!

Open arms and affectionate endearments set the stage for pleasant encounter back into the milieu instigating moist eyes and sobs. The ambient atmosphere appears different and the salient features responsible for pronouncing intrinsic dramaturgy just scant months ago now appear devoid of overarching sentimental gush! Common- place and regular objects just recently lorded over as cherished, priceless, rare and valuable items, now seem like quaint bric a brac! Alteration in perception the adequate explanation for such diminution in glorification of blood bonds sharing habitation, and edification from halls of education serves induction into karmic fortification!

Extrinsic credentials gathered from the fruits of labor applicable either to ambition and motivation to succeed in the classroom or even acceptance of non-skilled jobs distant from native turf. Both these hierarchically disparate choices imply that labors of love be adopted to benefit from cleansing process (comparable to immersion into the baptismal waters) to wash away traces of feverish longing and pangs indicative of beloved home sickness syndrome. The courage to make numerous attempts against weak-kneed vulnerability grants liberation against omnipotent ties that bind and subsequently injects boost to ego. Empowerment and self-actualization raise confidence. Self-esteem basks in a radiant glow, which outshines porch lights of yesterday.

Future paved with irresistible and intangible benefits that no beseeching hands from mama or papa can challenge. Utilitarian skill sets incontrovertibly trump the original habiliment that circumscribes and describes growing up phase, and underscores the message that one cannot go back from whence they came!

By Matthew Scott Harris

Introspection is a Bear

Introspection is a bear that takes its time to recognize when it has awakened from its sleep. It's eyes moving across the memory of landscapes that bristle and tickle its fur as its attention stirs up perception to repeat again. The bees and butterflies fuss and frolic about their daze and sometimes stumble across a bear. Why one bee darts away and one butterfly floats around to see what can be seen, I cannot say. It may be that a bee feels stung by another and the butterfly playfully tickles along its way. Each brings a different experience to the bear and so they often get very different outcomes.

When introspection lays its head down to follow its dream it forgets that it is part of the experience. As the dream plays with the dreamer, introspection will wander through wonders. All the time asking, "I wonder what this could be?"

By Joseph A. Santiago

Monologue Number One

The daily drama of my life finds this mister mom capering to and fro (like some frenetic flying germane Dutchman) in his trademark comedic madcap slapdash attempt to prepare my deux daughters for school!

Take this morning for instance!

A typical day here in the Harris household usually finds the eldest progeny (Eden Liat) shaking sleep from her petite twelve year old body!
She relies on this papa to prepare her lunch.

Dada neither bright eyed nor bushy-tailed but only barely awake before this first born, I asked if the menu of pasta with butter sprinkled with Parmesan cheese (kept warm in a thermos) would suffice.

The lack of any verbal objection is interpreted as an affirmative answer. Dialogue prior to when the older or younger ready themselves to wait for the bus frequently is communication via basic animal groans and/or grunts, with every now and again an objectionable exclamation hurled at the other sibling or even (gasp) at this father figure!

He (meaning the author of this brief ordinary family routine) does not react when either one or the other lass acts outside the paradigm of ladylike propriety, as he realizes that the being abruptly jarred from deep sleep (akin to getting rattled in a bell jar) does affect a tempest in a teapot temperament!

Once the girls have scurried off to yet another day of learning, I will shutter myself (like a bug snug in a rug) and meditate with an attempt to escape (albeit temporarily) the travails of this less than optimal existence!
Within the quiet mindful lightness of my being, the cogs and wheels of me noggin turn and try to gear up for the regular series of challenges!
While immersed in this shut-eye slightly hypnotic self induced state flashes of insight to strike in an effort to ponder how solution per the following grievances against us!

Why in the name of tarnation must we be plagued with a. exponential growing living costs primarily (impossibly to afford) taxes; b. financial woes; c. pestilential threats from the in-laws who demand we leave with little recourse to live elsewhere; d. residential repairs that continually get deferred to some unspecified future date; e vehicular malfunctions – namely that check engine light glaring frightfully, to name four issues that fester within the body, mind, and spirit triage of this fellow!

In addition to the tribulations from monetary shortcomings (sole income based on social security disability due to generalized anxiety), figuratively getting battery acid from Zison triumvirate, saggy square of ceiling plus wiggly door handle that does not lock, and lastly difficulty to afford another automobile (to replace the 1995 Subaru Legacy), prompts temptation to stay hidden under the blankets for an eternity!

By Matthew Scott Harris

My Story of Mental Health and Mindfulness

I want to show people that there is another way to live. And that you don't have to listen to what you're told to do. You can make up your own life - your own way of living. Don't ever think that you have to do things the way other people have done them before you. Find your own path. Do it your own way. Do what feels right for you.

When I was first diagnosed with bipolar depression it wasn't a surprise to me. Although I had no idea what that was, I knew something unhealthy was going on inside of me. I was unhappy and had felt that way for most of my life. Not that I couldn't remember times when I had fun and did feel happy, but they never lasted very long and were always followed by bits of anguish and downward spirals.

Depression was an ugly word I hated to hear and it took me a while to actually admit to my mom that I was depressed. That was the hardest thing for me, opening up. I didn't want to let anyone in on how I was feeling because I didn't want to bother anyone else with my problems. I guess I felt as though it was my struggle, my cross to bear, and only I was supposed to deal with it. Plus I didn't really even understand much of what was going on inside me, and explaining to others seemed like an impossible task. So I held it all within. I kept all the thoughts, feelings, and emotions locked up inside of me. They were like a ticking time bomb waiting to explode. They ate away at me inside and made me question everything, even life itself.

Let's just put this out right now. I wanted to die. I didn't want to be alive. To me all the pain I felt inside wasn't worth it. I wanted to escape and be free from the suffering. And at those times in my life, the only solution I could see was death itself. Luckily for me, what I consider my biggest fault, indecision, became the factor that saved my life. Ironically, I just couldn't commit to being so unhappy with my life to be convinced enough to want to end it. So fortunately I never tried. But despite all the negativity I experienced and created for myself, I still had this undying optimism and will to stay alive. Although it would be masked during times of depression, it was still there. I felt and still do feel there is a reason I am here on this planet especially at this time, and ending my own life would be selfish, inconsiderate, and above all else ungrateful.

After years of on and off depressions and great inner chaos, I had a huge breakdown. About a week before my 18th birthday, I took off in my car with intentions of not returning. I was initially contemplating suicide that night but luckily decided against it. Instead I was going to run away. I had my own car that I paid for (although still in my mother's name) and enough money in the bank. I was headed southbound for Florida. I was speeding like crazy, selfishly risking the life of myself and others, but I didn't care. I just needed to get away and I needed to get away fast.

A miracle happened that night or I would like to call it that. I got all the way to New Jersey in only a couple hours and despite the fact that I had only a little less than half a tank of gas left, I felt the need to stop and get more. Right after I crossed the George Washington Bridge I stopped but for some odd reason as I went to use the ATM, it wouldn't let me take out any money. So I went to the next gas station and tried again – still no luck. I tried another gas station . I even had my pin written down on a piece of paper in my car and took it out to make sure I was entering the right pin. I held it directly in front of me while entering it into the ATM – still no luck. It was getting really weird . I must have tried stopping at least four different gas stations before I decided that there was no other option but to turn around and go back home. Fortunately, I made it home safe that night with literally just enough gas. If there are such things as guardian angels or spiritual beings looking out for us, there must have been one following me that night.

The next day, with the support of my mother, I admitted myself to the hospital for suicidal depression. They sent me to the psychiatric ward of Fatima Hospital and unexpectedly the weight was temporarily lifted off my shoulders. There I was diagnosed as bipolar and put on a medication made of lithium. This was supposed to stabilize my moods --funny because it is the same medication they use to prevent seizures. I stayed there for a week, spending my 18th birthday locked up in a psych ward. But the toughest thing was getting out – going back into the world. At first it was liberating - like I had a new me, a second chance. But then it set in. I had to figure out how I was going to live my life healthy and happy, not depressed and suicidal anymore. I had to learn how to live again, in a different, healthier way than before.

They told me that bipolar is a progressive disorder and that one in four people end up committing suicide (if untreated). They said that I would most likely have to be on medication for the rest of my life –medication that they weren't exactly sure was going to work. Sometimes the medication makes it worse and can make people even more depressed, crazy and suicidal - one of the reasons I never trusted the medication to begin with. I knew that it didn't feel right, at least not for me. I still took the medication for a year after that.

Back home, a psychiatrist put me on another medication as well to "chemically boost my overall well-being." I thought I'll try them for now and see what happens, see if they help. And honestly, to this day I'm not sure I can say they did.

The following fall, I went away to a school in Florida kind of spontaneously and somewhat out of whim. I had initially planned to go to URI my first semester, and then transfer there. But I made a last minute decision and headed there for my freshman year. I took part in ROTC –the military officer training program they offer at colleges. I was part of the student government. I pledged a sorority. I was active in other clubs and of course went out and partied. I had tons of fun, and accomplished a lot but at the same time being down there was extremely tough; especially since I hadn't taken full responsibility for my mental health. I was avoiding being honest with myself. I mean, I was taking my medication still, but doing nothing else to really deal with the depressions and moods. And it would get confusing because sometimes I'd be fine and other times I wouldn't. I would think, "OK nothing to worry about" and I'd forget about healing myself. Then I'd get depressed and couldn't accomplish much. It was on and off but that is the nature of being bipolar.

Eventually I came to the conclusion that I didn't feel comfortable being on medication anymore. I think it was when I started to realize I wasn't remembering my dreams. Dreams have always been very interesting and valuable to me and sacrificing that wasn't an option I wanted to pursue. So I slowly weaned myself off the pills and started my journey of doing things naturally. I had always believed in the power of thought and intention and the human capability to heal. To me, I saw that as a personal task placed into my life. I saw my condition as being bipolar and being depressed not as just a chemical thing, but a creation of the environment I was brought up in. And I felt as though if I was really going to heal myself, I wanted to do it right – not cover up the symptoms of the condition with drugs.

I didn't really know where to start at first because no one knew what I was attempting to do. I stayed there the whole year, struggling with school and whether I wanted to stay, always questioning everything. I went back the following fall and became even more active in my sorority and student government. But again I was avoiding getting down to business with my mental health. I eventually came to a point at the end of the semester where I decided that I needed to take some time off from school and go home for a little bit. This way it would give me enough time to do some research on dealing with being bipolar in natural ways, and could figure out some things regarding school. I was just so confused with everything and the confusion brought me down even further. It made me hopeless because I was stuck.

This indecision and lack of confidence in my choices continued and still continues to create issues in my life. But like everything, it is just another thing I am learning to improve.

One of the first things that I found for natural depression remedies for bipolarity was meditation. I had heard about it before but didn't really know what exactly it was. So I did some more research. I learned and practiced and honestly had a lot of fun while struggling to learn to meditate. It was a whole new world which promised benefits beyond anything else. What was awesome about getting into meditative practices was not just the experience of feeling calm and relaxed afterwards, but the whole awareness and mindfulness concepts that came along with it. I can say without a doubt that learning how to harness and control my mind, instead of letting my mind control me, has been one of the most useful and beneficial tips for dealing with depression and bipolar disorder. It was really very amazing actually. When you're taught by people who have gone to school for years and years that you have to stay on medication, or else you'll end up committing suicide, or your condition will progress and get worse, to learn that all that is not true is startling. Yes, the condition may be medically proved to be a chemical imbalance, but medication is not the only answer. I believe anything is possible, and I especially believe that we have the power to heal ourselves. It's all about awareness of our thoughts and emotions. I felt that this awareness could be used to change my mentality and improve my mental health. And I can say that it really did.

Now, I'm not saying as soon as I learned about the mind and how to control my thoughts and emotions I got completely better. Even after that semester off of wonderful discoveries and dramatic improvement, I still suffered from depressions where I was somewhat suicidal , although not as intensely and not for as long as when I was younger. I was slowly making steps closer to where I wanted to be. Thinking that it was all going to go away right away would have been unrealistic. I now can say that I have improved dramatically. When I get depressed enough to question life which happens very rarely, I come to grips much faster and move forward quicker. Without question, meditation and mindfulness have been some of the major factors for improving my mental health. And the best part is I am learning to be happy with wherever I am on this journey of self-discovery. I can't turn around now, I've made it this far and I can't wait to see what my future holds.

By Chelsea Longa

Snake: A Christmas Shopping Story

I didn't want to do it. My mother made me. Well, she didn't say I had to, exactly. She kept saying, like, how much it would mean to my aunt, and how much my aunt had done for me, and she sighed this little sigh that she does – you know, the one that means, "a good person would do this, and if you don't do it I'll have to ask myself what I've done wrong in raising you." Your mother does that, too. I've heard her.

So, anyhow, the thing with my aunt is this. She used to be a teacher, and she was pretty much up on all the latest. She was tuned in. She knew what kids like. But then she got this other job being a technical writer for this big company, which pays way more money, but she never sees any kids anymore. So she's, like, clueless. It's not like she's forgotten. But she left off being a teacher before I was born, so, the kids she was tuned into are all grownups by now. It was a whole other world. So Mom sent me to help her with her Christmas shopping.

So here's my aunt. She comes and picks me up and she's like, isn't this wonderful, we have this time for bonding. She doesn't come out and say this but she smiles like she's too glad to see me, and you can just tell she's thinking what a good time she's going to give me, so on top of everything she and of course Mom will want me to act sort of thrilled.

So we go to the mall, and I swear, we're dragging around that place for hours. You never realize how many steps it is from one end to the other until you do it with an aging relative in tow. And she really doesn't like stuff all that much. Like the clothes. She's thinking maybe she can just get the twins Shetland sweaters in good primary colors, you know? A size too big, so they can grow into them and get more wear out of them. But what we find are all these Polartec pullovers in like chartreuse and orange and purple. They're warm and they have this feature where they wick out the water, so the kids stay cozy even in the rain, but she kind of shakes her head.

And she doesn't like the toys all that much either. She kind of looks wistful and says, "Blocks." And I go, "Blocks?" And she says, "Yeah, blocks. You could make them into anything at all – all you needed was imagination and a bunch of wooden blocks." And I go, "Well, look at this – it's a three-dimensional jigsaw puzzle, you put it together and it's a castle – over a thousand pieces. It will challenge the twins' spatial reasoning skills." And she shakes her head and goes, "That's too bad. They have to make it into what it wants to be, not what they want it to be. And they have to get it right. Not very forgiving, is it?" And she keeps looking for truly boring stuff.

So finally we break for lunch, and I'm almost done, but she still hasn't bought much of anything. We stop at the Newport Creamery, and then we have to go to the ladies' room, and I finish first & wash up and go stand just outside the door to make room, you know how crowded those places can get. And this really sullen-looking girl goes in there. I think nothing of it until I hear my aunt scream, "My snake!" So the girl comes rushing out with my aunt's bag, and I sort of block her way and stick out my foot to trip her, and my aunt is in there – still pulling up her panties I think – and she's yelling, "My snake! Give me back my snake!" and the girl is stumbling past me and getting away when all of a sudden this snake head comes up from my aunt's bag and just sort of looks around. The girl screams and drops the bag and runs out of there really fast. By this time everybody else is running at me and the bag. The manager and a real big waiter apprehend me, like I was the thief, and my aunt has to vouch for me, and the snake slithers deeper into the bag for cover and they don't seem to notice it, and my aunt is thanking them all over the place, so I wait until we get outside and then I ask, "What's a snake doing in your handbag, anyhow?"

"Oh," she goes, "it's not real. It's in beta testing. I've got the remote in my pocket, see?" So she hands me this little thing and I start pushing buttons and sure enough the snake comes up and he looks all around and wiggles and you really have to be pretty close up to tell he's not real.

And, I mean, she's asking *me* what the twins would like for Christmas? The woman is clueless.

By Gale Eaton

Speaking to My Future Self

I'm keeping secrets from myself. Right now I'm imagining how it might go down as I have explain the reasons that it took longer than we decided to get to where we wanted to be. How these momentary distractions that litter every moment of the day are the challenging tools that will be used to shape or break the gift of our ultimate vision. Right now I'm doing things that will almost completely be forgotten by my future self a year from now. There is so much that we both have agreed to let lapse into the haze of time and memory. Yet just because I can't remember it all doesn't change the sum of so many moments that supports me so that I can embrace what is here now. In each self that develops there always seems to be a crossroads that links our ideas to elements so that one day someone might say that we have stepped upon a new path. The strange irony is that we do not have to see ourselves multiplied to discover that many of our actions do not work in harmony with our intent. I write these words to ask my future self to keep reaching. I write these words to give myself a record that I can look back on to see how far we've come. A great thing happens when I put my thoughts and goals down on paper. I look back on what I wrote and it seems as if the potential I sought has always been there.

By Joseph A. Santiago

Surfacing Music

I hear the word music and my first impression is an instrument pressed tightly against a breast as fingers stroke, pluck, strum, and slide across strings. I imagine each note produced as a colored wispy wave appearing like smoke drifting away from its source in slow visible traces. Different speeds of notes colliding with environmental static to focus harmonic geysers washing over everything in range. Colors of wispy melodies run smooth and strike against my body every second of the day to stimulate the energies like sand upon a shore. It can all wear me down.

Listening to the constant chatter inside me and surrounding me, I find that voices become like music. Words are forgotten and the rhythm, pace, and tones, all become the melody that sway me silently to relax or quicken my heart so that I seek to drive forward with each step. As words are forgotten, I move with the rhythms repeating the sounds with my mind's intimate echo, my mind constantly hoarding every peep, pop, and whistle, to play out again long after the musician is gone. The voices of my past may argue or sing all to have a chance at becoming a sound so definitive it is shared to become never ending. Taking shape and turning on and off an emotional state that seems hard wired into my biology, I find myself believing that I am just one note in a building symphony calling out to all with its song.

By Joseph A. Santiago

The Cost of Anger

Anger...It's a blind emotion that turns and twists at the reality that we accept as whole. It takes the passions we love and cherish as it slowly turns them into the monsters from our nightmares. Where does it steam from? Who decided that anger would be so blinding? Does the human psyche give it the infinite power that dwells and lingers on our pallets like the taste of soiled milk? Slowly I can feel it linger in my subconscious, weighing down on my views and perspectives, as the people slowly around me turn into icons of cruel nature and devastation. This emotion, so deadly it was gifted in the bible with the name "wrath," lingers in my soul as the words of those around me tingle and pick at it like a child picking at a scab. The senses tell the mind "no," but the body reacts without thought. Does this make me a cruel person? I look at the pictures of my family and linger on the conversations where the words seemed flooded with malice and acid, which rip at my brain leaving small cuts and aches where points of pleasure should be. Why do they speak of such insolence? Do they not see the world around them is changing? Even I, one stuck in the past, can look through the mirror beyond traditions and understand.

Looking at the faces as the future of the world plays out as the youths of our times turn and pillage in the streets. Their signs beg for freedom, their flags shimmering in the classic "R-O-Y-G-B-I-V" that we grew up learning in art classes. Do their colors make them wicked? Anger floods my soul once more as those around them scream and rant about their misdeeds. What have these youths done but speak for themselves, begging for the right to free love? What misdeeds have they committed? No blood lingers on their finger tips. Who has sinned? Death to those who leave the light of God, yet it make me wonder if God had wished such things be done in his name. Civil rights is nothing but the past repeating itself. Color being blinded and ignored. How much death will it take this time, before it's decided we were wrong? What does this show for the future? Will change be a constant battle that once again floods the streets with corpses of brothers, sisters, mothers, and fathers? When will we learn that change doesn't always need death to follow in its stead?

Looking down at the books that had been accepted and used on countless occasions nowhere does it state particular requirements. beside "love." Nowhere does it state that one cannot love another simply because they are the same. Who are we fighting? Looking down the streets as the colors march my heart begins to proudly beckon, screaming as the voices of ignorance are the ones the world listens to. Voices of destruction, voices of pain, anger once more...Acid burning away at the inside of my heart, as it slowly longs to possess my body, when will this nightmare end? It makes me wonder how someone cannot love another simply because of their birth right to love another. How can a family look towards a youth and decide they are unworthy? What is worth? Does it really exist? Or is it like anger, something we give more power than it actually holds. Such power we give ourselves. Such great commands as we look down on those who love differently then us, who look different then we do. When will we finally cast aside the anger, cast aside the toll of death, and learn that Race is a title, and the only race in the world is human. Once the world looks beyond the labels instilled to give those who use them power, we will finally be able to love without boundaries. In a world where everyone is free to fly.

By Alexandra Epervary

The Inconceivable Finish

I grew up in Norwalk, Connecticut as a member of the American underclass. My mother was 19 and unwed when I was born; my family was poor; my social position was such that I was very unlikely indeed to end up at the age of 21 presenting a paper at the 7th International Congress of Qualitative Inquiry. How I grew up, and how I improbably ended up here, is the subject of this presentation.

I spent most of my childhood, thinking I was born just as "equal" as everyone else, with notions that "justice" was inevitably equal for everyone. It was consistently recited to me as a young child that everyone is created equal, and that I could be anything I set my mind to be. It was nice advice throughout my childhood, but it turned out not to be true. I was taught that everyone is created equal, and it's what you do with your life in society that sets you apart from others-- given the right opportunity that is. But the problem with opportunities is they come around more often for some over others, depending on social class. There is a barrier that separates someone who lives their life, no matter the circumstances, to the best of their ability to strive upwards in the stratification system, compared to persons among the social elite, who are placed on a road without the same restrictions.

These social elites don't have to abide by what is considered a "just" lifestyle. Elites are able to uphold an identity that constructs a "being" among the bourgeoisie, meaning elites in our society can pave their own road by ignoring social equality, because they make the rules of the game. They are able to appear as caregivers, when actually they constitute a global bureaucracy which feeds people what passes as a healthy nutrient, but is actually a fat that clogs the arties of humanity over a long period of time. The truth is in order for the socially fabricated embedded royalist factions to remain on top, social control of the underclass has to be established and maintained.

As I look back on my life, I see the opportunities I was presented with unfold before my eyes, but I was too blind to see as they came along that it wasn't entirely me that created them. Society's institutions and ideologies become "normalized" in consciousness, which manipulates people's beliefs in line with their social identities. The insecurities created by these arrangements work as a tool to keep the "serpent-like" system in constant movement, adjusting to any hiccup, all to benefit the people who govern the "machine" that runs according to social class. Being labeled as "on welfare" or as "criminal" hinders people's impressions of themselves, along with the way others look upon them. Society uses these measures to cause people to look down on themselves, to not pursue social improvement, but to remain in the social class position they are in. Words such as "gang member", "welfare", or "criminal" are associated with underclass identities, which carry a burden of negativity in society.

The key to decipher society's codes is knowledge. Education is the key to place all social classes on a more even keel, giving more people a fair shot in an unfair situation. I was an only child sharing a bedroom with my mom for the first 6 years of my life at my grandparent's house. The room had two twin beds located on each side of the room. We both had a dresser for our clothes. There was a television and a small closet. My mom gave birth to me at age nineteen. My biological father was twenty-nine at the time. So I started out in my home town of Norwalk, Connecticut living with my mom, grandmother, grandfather, an aunt, an uncle, and two family friends, all in one house. The house was fairly large, and the day we left there was a tragic day for me. I had a place where all my toys fit into one large walk-in closet, and I enjoyed the big yard I was able to hit a ball around in. But when I was four we moved to another house off a main road further into the city where the rent was cheaper. I now lived only with my mom and grandparents, but I still had to continue to share a bedroom with my mom.

I managed to go to three elementary schools over the course of two years, where I took constant ridicule for being the fattest child (obese children are, of course, common in the American underclass). I was dealing with this issue at school, and home wasn't much better. My grandfather was a full blown alcoholic who would verbally abuse the family. I actually thought it was fun to call the police when things got out of hand. It was like a version of cops and robbers, which I used to play at after school. I picked up on things my grandfather would say and used them towards my mom and grandmother. I used to refer to them as "woman" instead of "mom" or "nana". I would fight over my mom's attention, because she would go out a lot, trying to live the young adult life. I slept most of the time on the couch, and wet the bed quite frequently. I would sneak by my grandfather who would be up all night watching "Married With Children" and "Law and Order", constantly coughing. I would tap my grandmother on the foot to signal her that I needed her assistance. It actually made me feel safe that my grandfather was up late at night and that I wasn't all alone. I went on living with them until I was seven, but the fear of sleeping alone never did quite go away.

So, at this time, I categorized a certain type of person as alcoholic. Every forty- year-old that drove a tractor-trailer and wore a hat everyday was an alcoholic to my eyes. I never considered in that time period that an alcoholic could be anyone no matter their job or social class. The image that was presented to me on a daily basis was only him; I was never fed an alternative view, so I categorized all people who fit his image as alcoholic. The same can be said for images portrayed as "criminal" or "gang member". People are fed socially what these two labels are supposed to look like. This labeling makes for unfair treatment for many people who are in fact not criminals or gang members, placing them in groups that are looked at as inferior. People in power positions want to induce fear to socially segregate groups out of mainstream society. This social mechanism results in more opportunities for the socially defined superior groups.

I ended up moving out of that second house with my grandparents and mom into another apartment across town away from my grandparents. I lived on the top floor of a two family house with my mom. My aunt and uncle lived downstairs. I had another case of fearing the unknown during the move, and also when I was told I had to switch schools once again. We moved into a section of town where we were one of the very few white families around. I lived in a home that had no heat in the winters; I had to put plastic tape around the windows to keep warm. I was given the opportunity to go to the "rich school" that was further away from the school where the majority of kids I lived around were sent. It was worked out with the school administration and my mom that I could attend the upper class school out of my district if I was able to find my own transportation there. I never asked questions, but was just glad to have friends to play ball with after school away from the isolation I felt at home. If I was riding in a car by my neighborhood with friends from my school I would tell them to duck down, because we might get shot at by the people in the ghetto. The chances of that happening were slim to none, but I wanted to accumulate myself into the social class I interacted with for a majority of my time.

I used to ask myself why no other kids were given the same opportunity to go to the predominately white school. This school had a bigger playground, lots of field trips, and the teachers were always available. Most of the women in that area were housewives who were always able to chaperone. My mom rarely had the time to take off work to do so. On Christmas some years I was asked to come down to the office were I was given a large bag full of toys and school supplies. I was still in elementary school at this point and thought school was great. My mom would tell me, "Michael, be grateful for what you are, not many kids that live around you are going to get the same opportunity". I tried to fit in as hard as I could with the kids who were members of the beach club and wore Jordan's. I did not know what Jordan's were and went to school in a pair of shoes I bought at "payless shoes" with a picture of Michael Jordan on the side of them. I still had to deal with the comments about being overweight and poor. I always battled to fit in, but realized that it was better not to get too attached, and instead search for what felt right socially. I spent a lot of time around family and teachers.

My teachers called me a slow learner, but I had great friends that helped. I also took part in as many school activities available to me. If it wasn't white, I know I would not have been given the same treatment being from a ghetto area where there was little opportunity for upward mobility. Even as a little kid I could tell that the setting at school was drastically different than my home. I remember I used to barricade my door at night with all the toys in my toy box just in case someone tried to break in. There were instances where my mom's car was robbed, as well as my aunt's apartment downstairs. I always felt safer at school or at my grandparents. I was like a FedEx package for the number of households to which I would be shipped off to sleep over, because either my mom was working or went out for the night.

Education was more accessible for areas that were rich and had resources, not just because of race, but because of a combination of institutions that set some areas up for success. Schools without these advantages failed to receive the funding needed to be on an equal status. To me this wasn't fair for everybody, so I chose to play for the baseball team close to my house, rather than play for the school. Somehow, I knew at a young age not to fall into the trap society sets up for you, but to judge everyone on who they are regardless of their class or cultural background.

Still, my elementary school gave me an opportunity in fifth grade to do a week program for free with the local police department, at a National Guard base to learn about substance abuse and team activities. It was a program that took inner city kids out of their environment to educate them about substances, and build teamwork through many activities. It was also set up to implement discipline. For instance, at night in our bunks, if people were loud when the lights went out, we were directed outside to do push-up's. I remember we had to walk four miles to the beach as a group. My friend from my neighborhood could not walk anymore because of the heat, so I took the initiative to carry him to the beach. I just did it, but it won me the leadership award. To me it was a fun weekend, but it was foolish to think a weekend away was going to change our lives forever. A weekend later, we were back in the same setting where we started before we boarded the bus. This shows that a lot of the resources used to educate kids from poor areas must remain consistent, and cannot be on a one and done basis.

While I was given opportunities at school, it was a different matter when it came to health insurance. My mom was on welfare and was receiving very little from my biological dad. I had to go only to certain doctors and dentists who accepted welfare. I remember my mom always looking through the phone book to find out who did accept our insurance. Once, when I was eight, I went to the dentist from an upper class town that bordered my town. I always got nervous around any type of doctor. He told me to sit in the chair, and told my mom to leave the room. I started to cry and he told me to "shut up". I continued to cry so he choked me and forced my mouth open. My mom said later that she did not come in because the secretary told her everything was fine. After the visit I told my mom what happened and we went the local police where they took pictures and interviewed me. They asked if I could tell the difference between a story and the truth. I insisted that I was attacked by the dentist and they told me they would look into in, like I was making everything up. I felt I was treated very unfairly during this process. It was later found out that this dentist treated many other welfare cases similarly. It was a simple case of punishing the poor. This seems to be a major theme in our society. The groups of people who do not fit the standards for valuable human beings are treated differently, are exploited, because to the society's privileged they are of no value and beneath respect.

I realized early that the way to keep moving was education. After a graduation party at my friend's house everyone was talking about what middle schools they were going to attend. Many of the kids were off to private middle schools and I felt left out. I mentioned this to my Godmother who picked me up that day, and she said she might be able to arrange an interview for a private catholic school in my town. I went to the school to introduce myself to the principal. They told me what the school offered and how it worked. I told them about my situation and my hobbies. The only issue I had was the price of tuition. Luckily I was able to obtain a fifteen thousand dollar scholarship through the school to attend there all three years. I was so excited to be accepted because I knew that friends from my elementary school were going there as well. This was also the first time I had to wear a suit to school. This is the time I began the transformation from one social class up to the next. I also did not have to get my own transportation to school, because a bus would pick me up in my neighborhood.

My mom had met my future step-dad and we were looking for a new home. I ended up moving to the place I am still living at today, a place were I had my own room and a yard back. My mom finished school and got a good job. We now had good health insurance. I finished up my three years at middle school and was off to high school. I was offered another great opportunity to continue going to a catholic school, but I turned it down because most of my friends were going to the public high school this time around. I was on my way to places I never knew were out there.

High school was a different world for me, and I found myself in search of my own identity. I was able to observe a more diverse social setting in a public school; I played football and made a variety of friends. A problem arose in my sophomore year when I was diagnosed with a tumor in my neck. I had to go to the prestigious Yale New Haven Hospital to have it removed after months of research and analysis. I also was told that I did not owe anything for my massive surgery. My mom's new health insurance took care of it. I just remember thinking, "What if I was still on welfare?"

After the surgery, I had to wear a neck brace for four months and be home schooled. Teachers from my school came over to present me with homework and one on one teaching in my core subjects. During this hectic time I challenged myself not only physically, but academically. I was never a strong student on paper, because I still thought I was a slow learner. But during this time I showed myself that good grades were possible. I was treated with a lot of respect and class during this time. I could not help but think about the time spent at my old dentist's, and every time I stepped foot in a doctor's office. I noticed that I had started to move out of the underclass. I was in the process of finding my new role and hoped success was a part of it.

Like every high school kid I went through the phases of what to wear? Who to ask out? What car to drive? The most important thing I took from high school was I never got involved with just one clique. I was a roamer and was able to see how each group culturally fit. Each course level in school was still socially segregated. Each class had three levels based on performance. It was easy to see that the majority of poor white and minority kids were in the lower sections. I saw this as a lack of social justice. I was predominately in the higher sections, but never fully motivated to do well. I applied to some universities but decided that I was going to head towards community college first to get my feet wet.

Norwalk Community College is where I began my college journey. This was another school that had a large range of people. I knew it was time for me to step up to the plate and get ahead. I was dealing with issues outside of school and knew more doors would continue to open with education. My first semester at Norwalk Community College I earned a 4.0 grade point average which gave me the motivation to keep going. I dug in and became focused on being a student. I was inducted into Phi Theta Kappa, an international honor society for two year colleges. I later became the Vice President of the chapter. I implemented numerous outreach events for people around the community. Each semester I organized river cleans-up's near the "homes" of homeless people, as well as food drives for people and for animals. I did breast cancer walks for the American Cancer Association, and judged Keep American Beautiful contests. The two years spent at Norwalk made me grow as a person. I was a nursing major at the time, but when I was introduced to sociology, I truly made connections that brought the world around me, and the world I grew up in into perspective. I knew it was time for me to think about transferring. I decided to apply only to the University of Rhode Island, where I had been rejected out of high school. Three weeks later I received my letter of acceptance and it was official: I was going to the University of Rhode Island.

So I made it to a traditional four year institution. I am the first in my family to do so. I am grateful for the opportunities that have come my way, as well as for my family who supported me. Through my core classes in sociology, I became more tuned in to everything around me. I don't think I can look at anything anymore and not see how it relates back to sociology. I am picking up two additional majors along the way, Psychology and English. I am currently a teaching assistant and President of both the Sociology and Psychology clubs. I renamed the sociology club the "Iron Cage Society" in honor of Max Weber. As a friend of mine once said it's important to "Think big and follow through". I am determined to do that.

I am pleased to see that some people at URI, (including two of my roommates who come from the South Providence projects) are given an opportunity to be at college and away from the underclass life I once saw back home. But many get no such opportunity. There is a lot wrong with the system in place: it degrades people, and divorces them from their true potential at a young age, when it counts the most. Dividing social classes on fundamental levels like education, health insurance and security may serve some well, but it weakens the whole. As to the individuals, the way I look at it is it's not where you started, but where you finish. Martin Luther King once said that "the arc of the moral universe is long but it bends towards justice". I like to believe that is true and that it is in the people's hands to make that belief a reality. The most important thing is to take advantage of the opportunities we are presented with. It is our job as a society to create opportunities that work for the common good. There is always more than one right way of doing things that equals justice.

As I look back on the journey that has me standing in the position I am in right now, I reflect on the joy I feel every time I am able to put my best foot forward. This reflexive piece is to open the eyes of those not in on my life, and to use my life story as an example of the inequality and lack of social justice found in our society. I am grateful for the opportunities I have had, but would like to see many others have a shot at them as well. I truly feel that I was reborn many times in diverse situations. This poem attempts to capture that experience.

Joy

I'm the russet shriveled raisin,
the blemished pickle saturated in the salty brine of another.
Sitting suspended in waiting for a long anticipated liberation.
How long has it been, since I last saw my copious comrades?
Nine lengthy, prolonged months, marked with anticipation, hesitation.
For after my exodus, I must confess,
to the highest degree, it was my jubilee, to be finally free, from my prior,
confined dynasty.
Yet into another I would plunge,
The one I now consider my own abode.

I'm the pensive artist's unfinished canvas,
waiting to be crafted into a new solid form of my own.
I'm the anxious football,
feverish to be kicked betwixt the posts that mark victory to the one who
flung it.
Finally—movement.
And like a swift, fervent freight train,
I peel out from my dark cavernous residence,
plunging, penetrating this fresh exotic world.
It's all so alien—the lofty white entities flitting about, poking and prodding at
each and every faction of my being.
From arm to arm I'm accepted around this bright new-fangled home of mine.
When finally I find refuge in a small, supple nook, swaddled in the arms of a
compassionate smile, and a steady hand.
I'm the last patch, the final part to the whole quilt that is
my family.

By Michael Cichowicz

(This paper was presented at the Seventh International Congress of Qualitative Inquiry, University of Illinois, Champaign-Urbana, May 18—21, 2011.)

The River

When someone touches you in a way you didn't expect, don't understand, it changes you. Thoughts shape who we are; winding between us like a fresh breeze, pushing us towards our destination. Colors mount, creating shapes within us and showing others who we are inside.

Turn a corner, where are you? What is down there that calls us? How do you know you will recognize your destination when you get there?

Emotions gather outside the door, waiting to be let in. It's a party inside your head. The light shifts to dark; night is growing. Time slips through your hand like rough grains sand, lost to the river of remembrance.

Love grows in your soul, directing you. Turning you towards your dreams.

By Riley Davis

Traditional Family Culture: Mono vs. Poly Political Family Perspective

Recently with all the political campaigns airing their attack ads, campaign speeches, stating personal declarations of what they stand for, and spouting perspectives on how the current system is broken and how they know just the way to fix it, I have begun to question just what are the traditional cultural values that so many politicians cling to. The political wife is often held up to be an active partner with one of her goals being providing a good home (Kan, & Heath, 2006). While providing a good home is important, what I see is many people happy to use their partner's to say, "Look at me. I'm a good person just like you." What happens when the model of family presented turns out to be a minority percentage or even a lie perpetrated to get a position that a group or individual wants (Brancato, 2007)? The cultural stereotype of family used is often not blamed for being too narrow, but the person is blamed for their conduct and quietly is encouraged to seek the sidelines in the political arena.

In the sixth grade (somewhere in the 1980's) I can remember talking with friends in homeroom to discover I was one of the five kids in a class of approximately thirty whose parents were not divorced. Now in my thirties I am happy to say that my parents are still together and I am still a minority by this fact from most of the people I have met. In the 1990s, every state had made at least one or more legislative policy changes with the intent of influencing divorce and promoting marriages of two-parent families (Kickham, & Ford, 2009). How the divorces rates are tallied is also convoluted enough to say that these politicians are choosing the best figures possible when it comes to divorce rates.

According to Kickham and Ford (2009), the common practice of collecting data on divorce rates presently has each state relying on its counties to track the number of divorces granted, and aggregate figures based on the state's population estimates to derive the rate of divorces granted per 1,000 populations. The problem is that the states themselves do not collect this data and do not have a uniform format to record, organize, and communicate it. If there is no uniform way to communicate and store it we have to assume that much of the data is not reported, may be misrepresented, lost, and possibly ignored. These statistics are being used as proof by politicians and others that the conformity of an absolutely monogamous culture exists and that they are its figureheads (Montgomery, 2006).

Cooperation of individuals as well as how institutions and social systems are structured are all supported by the examples and processes from the people who are in positions of power. These people set themselves up to demonstrate that the meaning and negotiations of culture is meeting the majority of people's everyday needs (Montgomery, 2006). The socialization agents of the family and community reinforce identities and cultural roles through shared activities and behavioral presentations to communicate to others that they belong to a group (Arnon, Shamai, & Ilatov, 2008). By sharing in a common group membership people assume that they also share the same concerns, because they demonstrate an understanding of the concepts and preferences of that group (Gardiner, & Kosmitzki, 2008).

The group-relationship is to therefore support these items of culture and say that while people may not be exactly monogamous, they can hold together a relationship consisting of two people at a later time. Once kids come into the picture it is almost never going to be just two people involved in raising children. If both parents who are divorced move on to other relationships then their significant others also play a part in that child(s) upbringing. This also adds more grandparents and possible new environments. It seems to me that while many people are still talking about a single monogamous unit of parenting that they should be talking about poly-committed relationships that include extended families.

The idea of having 2.5 children and a partner that stays at home maybe a good one but it is not a reality today for the majority of people. Finding time to spend with the family is the norm for everyone I know, and it is the same for most people across America (Melli, & Brown, 2008). The literature seems to suggest that there is no one best way to support our children, but it does seem to establish a need to encourage them in the many structural family forms. A poly culture can be seen through the many roles and relationships that we all must take to answer the needs of our daily life. Having one job over the course of the lifetime seems to be as rare as having one marriage partner in my experience.

Arnon, S., Shamai, S., & Ilatov, Z. (2008). Socialization agents and activities of young adolescents. Adolescence, 43(170), 373-397. Retrieved from CINAHL Plus with Full Text database.

Brancato, J. (2007). Domesticating Politics: The Representation of Wives and Mothers in American Reality Television. Film & History (03603695), 37(2), 49-56. Retrieved from Communication & Mass Media Complete database. Gardiner, H. & Kosmitzki, C (2008). Lives across cultures, cross-cultural human development. Boston, MA. Pearson Education, Inc.

Kaminski, M. (2010). L'Affaire to Remember. New Republic, 241(7), 9-10. Retrieved from Academic Search Complete database.

Kan, M., & Heath, A. (2006). The Political Values and Choices of Husbands and Wives. Journal of Marriage & Family, 68(1), 70-86. doi:10.1111/j.1741-3737.2006.00234.x.

Kickham, K., & Ford, D. (2009). Are state marriage initiatives having an effect? An initial exploration of the impact on divorce and childhood poverty rates. Public Administration Review, 69(5), 846-854. doi:10.1111/j.1540-6210.2009.02034.x.

Melli, M., & Brown, P. (2008). EXPLORING A NEW FAMILY FORM - THE SHARED TIME FAMILY. International Journal of Law, Policy & the Family, 22(2), 231-269. doi:10.1093/lawfam/ebn002.

Montgomery, A. (2006). Polyamorous Ideology: Democracy and Power in Intimate Life. Conference Papers -- American Sociological Association, 1. Retrieved from SocINDEX with Full Text database.

By Joseph A. Santiago

Life by Association

It does seem that every day we build upon the illogical logic that we believe to be absolute and real. Yet if we attempted to question everything that we know and how we know it we would go a bit more mad. It seems then that humans as social animals are dependent upon creating the most honest and logical environment and culture as possible to ensure that we do not fall prey to own illusions. While looking out at the world I know this is not what is going on, and so I struggle to ask a better question to answer why this isn't so. Even in the absence of true information my conscious mind has already thought up reasons why this could be so. In the end I am unsure that rational is honestly rational beyond the social agreements that we believe it to be. It does seem that the illogical is just as valued as the logical ideas at times. A circle of thoughts it seems...

O

One of the hardest things for me to learn as a writer and a human being was that I cannot wait for inspiration and conditions to be perfect before I start to work on what I love. There is always so much to do and it is easy to should on yourself until there is little energy left. When there are those moments where I have been lucky enough to be able to express myself through my work I have been reminding how much working on my own creativity moves me. I feel like my whole world gets a little bit better. Every day I strive and reach for even a gradual bit of improvement in doing what I love. Writing is a big part of it and because I want to do it I do not find the work to be a struggle. I do find it to be challenging and I want to laugh, cry, and even scream at times. When it comes to seeing how the final product comes out I feel like I can trace its evolution through the new ideas that I can see where always there in front of me. Do not wait for your inspiration to come to you through ideal conditions because what I have found is silence leaves me thirsty. Silence leaves me waiting and waiting and all that it would have taken was for me to start work. To allow myself to play with the elements that I love and the gift that I have received is my own voice. Imagine a world where everyone can share more of what they love and let's share with each other all that we have done. There is so much more that we can imagine and we cannot taste the richness of this life without sharing what we love. So sleep fast, love proudly, live well, and share your voice!

O

Compete with yourself because the many trials and challenges of focus and vision that nobody sees will be where you get to notice what you yourself can achieve. In the end all of us have to judge for ourselves what is true and worthwhile. Many people have told me numerous things about what is good and what is a successful. The only way to have another person know that they can invest in me or my work is to share with them the difference between what makes a person satisfied and what makes them loyal to an idea and a person. The difference in feeling is so profound that this one choice can make a person feel great throughout their life time. Everyone knows they can find something that will do the job for the moment. What gets people to listen and invites them to walk with us is passion that leads to commitment. The only way I have ever been able to compete with myself is to give more and to strive to better the expectation and the experience that I intend to share with others. I believe that no matter what a person's talk or walk may be it will be the quality of emotion and experience that can be delivered and shared with another that tells me I am a success.

O

The virtue of a good surprise is fusing it with swift secrecy and a catchy jingle. Everyone should have some theme music in their heads for moments like these.

O

Everyday there are more and more globalized business spreading their culture with their goods throughout the world. I have yet to see any organizational ethics or cultural expectations that seek to accept and include the concerns of everyone in their organization equally. I see that multiethnic and multinational corporation are embracing more of the local cultures but the organization as a change agent seems to be developing from a condition of tribalism to a participatory culture. Yet, to establish universal ethnical principles there must be more of a desire to understand and relate with one another. The idea that organizations operate in a vacuum has proved problematic for companies as the leaders that tend to seek that kind of perception tend to be setting the company up for a fall. As companies become more global entities I believe there will be many more conversations about the behaviors and ethics that companies support universally. The idea of universal ethics seems to be an impossible task until the human element is added. People will have different needs and seeking to invest in cultural practices will be what brings in market share globally. Brands are not just associations and ideals, they are being embraced as identities and lifestyles. The link between product, culture, and thought is being explored through our interactions every day. As organizations and company struggle to be the best they will seek to enhance our quality of life, promote environments that include their ideals, and ask us to listen how they can help to make us healthier. The human element is the global key to success and the great limiter on how fast and far.

O

Do most people really want to hear and know the truth? In the ancient past winners of an argument of debate were those individual's who were the most skilled in defining, shaping, and presenting their rational perspective frame over the topic or concern to convince the audience that the speaker had the best approach and understanding of the topic and its surrounding forces. The goal became to win regardless of truth and the greatest speaker could challenge a rival through the performance art of the presentation alone. The Greco-Roman method of debate can be seen today and just like in the past, it leaves the parties who did not receive the audience's favor scheming to take down the victor's position piece by piece if need be later. Innovation designed under the losing positions are often lost and ignored because conflict is often recognized as self-justification with the strongest owning the prize. Truth can too easily be ignored when if brings little favor until it brings enough suffering that a new head of truth emerges.

Each day people make countless choices and easily vacillate between reckless, routine, and trial and error styles of accepting/steering their present into their future. The influencing factors that flavor our perceptions include our personal and family history, cultural exposure, education (formal and informal), body image, feelings of attractiveness, social status, financial status, religion, health, fears, wants, desires, goals, biases, and so much more that creates the expectations and frames that label all that we see, feel, touch, and act upon as reality. Not only is that one long list, but it is not exhaustive nor exactly the same from person to person. By definition the way any of us will interact with each other will have to be through negation and to some degree conflict that starts at the level of perception. This doesn't even start to get into personal values, moral codes, laws, obligations, risk taking, or selfless and selfish acts. These are just rearranging the information and variables to do what we want or what we think is right. Yet how often does the average person step back to attempt to sympathize with another, or even to recognize that two or more positions may exist simultaneously without taking away the significance of the other.

Most problems are complex and have their roots running through cultural and societal traditions that have encompassed racial, ethnic, gender, familial, religious, and innovative squabbles that present unique expressions of identity and biases. The most persuasive leaders in the world have personal strengths that in some circumstances will be their personal liability. The willingness to open ourselves to better alternatives must also come with the intention of seeking and acknowledging our own biases and limitations. The responses I stimulate in another may be enough for today in one situation but can never represent nor recognize the whole creative truth and solution possible. What a person seeks to ignore or hide away always seems to have a way to come back to them. Even at the end of this rant I wonder how many people really seek out to know the truth so that they can best enhance their lives? I have seen over and over how willing some people are to tell me the truth as they see it. I want to know for myself if my reaction is towards the personality or the perspective that they seek to paint.

O

Today in this blended experience of digital and real world living everyone is seeking the feeling of intimacy through togetherness in face to face interaction and intimacy in the co-presence of interacting with others virtually. More and more each day I fold into my thoughts and at times my very DNA, how others experience and know the world. This voyeuristic modeling of vicarious experience allows me to learn so much more about my world and expand upon the concepts of community, relationships, and shared spaces, as I seek to develop myself with a seemingly unlimited array of talent to know. All relationships in this connected world view share spaces that are not limited by geography but the self-imposed limits of the language of expression and imagination. More and more everyday people are asking themselves where they want to go, who they are, and what is possible. Stop for a moment and imagine the future generations of people who are guided by the motivations of their hearts and minds. When so many of us carry devices that anchor us into multiple roles, discussions, and interactions, the only reason we have for doing something or not doing something will be Tweeted as our status soon enough. Perspectives on self-identity have been around for a long, long time, but social identity has in the past been tied to a geographic community. These free floating social spheres of influence seems closer to the mythic ideas of Olympus than the pedestrian routine interactions that so many people causally participate in. Presence now is part of impression management and the social self can be seen long after a person is passed on from this world. Like the myths Michael Jackson and Elvis still sing their songs to us, sometimes appear in games, commercials, and people continue to tell their stories. We are never alone takes on a new significance now compared to a hundred years ago.

O

Today, I feel that the purpose of my life is realize that everything encountered can be embraced to share and shape something from the goodness of who I am, and to tell you to be ready… because at any moment an unexpected touch can connect what we imagine with the amazing diversity of what we can encourage it to be.

O

In a warp and woof, the sine qua non, is how group form and tweet. Watching a public street seems to challenge the illusions of theory.

O

The best art takes routine reality by the knickers to surprise the observer and leave the view painted with the impressions of delight. The world somehow becomes art through this shared connection that reminds us that even we are more than we were a moment before.

O

I think we can only delight in helping other people when we are able to have fun playing fully with our self.

O

Craving something sweet and meaty… How does that work? Stress blahed!

O

I have learned that my silence just like my words can be regretted fiercely.

O

Enjoying writing about the aspects of cultural management that allow us to advertise our personal propaganda to establish social scripts!!

O

At Port City Java in NC I'm writing my heart out in an attempt to convince carbs and simple sugars to wait on the chair for the next guy to sit down.

O

And the Snow Queen became a story about seeking balance in one's life & not hurting the stranger who is shoveling snow behind her car...

O

Watching a person smile is like recognizing the light in the window of a warm soul. It communicates that can even from the coldest of nights we can approach and know that the heart is at home.

O

If we lie to ourselves long enough will the moment refuse to change?

O

It seems that even the gods have no answer for the temptations of love and the spoiled fruit that goes bad waiting upon the vine.

O

It's very possible in the future how people will identify will be part of a scale like this that shares their sex, sexual preference, and gender. For example I would be an MMMF. My sex is male, I identify as a man, my expression is masculine, and my sexual orientation is towards females.

This small step in specificity will make a difference for those people who feel that their gender does not match their sex. These people are often left behind and left out of many of the conversations that affect them as people on a daily basis.

O

People use stories to create the contexts for their lives so that the taste of experiences and challenges that are possible can be realized and shared with the desired intensity of spice.

O

I strive to craft ideas with my words to bridge peoples experiences not an ideal to dismiss conversation.

By Joseph Santiago

Photography by Amy M Serino

Wishing Flower

Closing

Thank you very much for enjoying this book. It is my hope that I can encourage people whose voices don't get heard to share their voice and know people are listening. I believe these books will inspire people to take an interest in their world, and create a dialogue about issues that affect us all. I would personally like to thank all the writers and artists that made this book and theme possible. Thank you again for your time, your support, and your feedback. We couldn't do this without you!

On Facebook as Joseph Santiago in the Providence, RI network
http://balanceheart.spaces.live.com
balanceheart@hotmail.com
http://twitter.com/World_Voice

All contributing authors in World Voice are hereby personally invited to join The World Voice Authors Circle. Please join us and be part of one of the largest network of authors, publishers, and employers from across the globe.

Please accept this invitation to join your group.
http://www.linkedin.com/e/gis/128926/69025934737C

Santiago Inc. Company Profile

Who are we?

Every day there is history being made and we all take part in it. Across geography and cultures many significant things have been lost, have been forgotten, or have systematically been buried and repressed. Through community building and culture exchanges, Santiago Inc. seeks to create partnerships and opportunities to learn from each other so that we might stop the erasure of our collective history. It is our hope that by connecting people globally, we will encourage the arts, promote cooperation, combat apathy, and support individuals in sharing their voice and experiences. In Joseph's words, "When we get together to share and write our experiences, we begin to see ourselves as individuals that are part of a constellation of culture and diversity instead of perceiving diversity as something that is separate from us and is acting upon our lives."

What do we do?

Santiago Inc. is a content production company and an independent publisher. The company develops and distributes documentary, cultural, educational, and informational reports, as well as entertainment, marketing and other content and service forms of print into the digital environment.

Why buy from us?

Santiago Inc. seeks more than profit. We have a mission that is meant to inspire others and enrich something larger than ourselves. Your purchase supports the endowment of a global culture reference, which works to further creative expression and mutual learning through the dream of inspiring others to take hold of their own creative capacity to better themselves and their world. Santiago, Inc. sees its works reaching beyond nationalities and borders to give a voice to those who labor to survive, live to love, support equality, explore and question, and extend the reach of organizations working to end repression, war, racism, poverty, and oppression. We seek to keep our costs low to provide an environment that allows all people equal access to our products and services. We do this work because it is a labor of love and a family business. We believe in what we do.

How does this benefit you?

When you buy a product or service from us we do not think of it as a one shot deal. Santiago Inc. strives to establish a lifelong relationship with each individual it serves. We do something different than any other publisher out there. We invite each person that buys a product or service to become part of the experience and knowledge that they invested in. Santiago Inc. wants you to share what you are passionate about as well as comment on what you think and suggest how we can improve. When we find information that adds value to our products and services we want to supplement our knowledge and perspectives to make our community better. Sharing your voice has the potential to shape the future and we may invite you to share your ideas by adding them into the next edition of published works. If you think you can do it better we will encourage that too! In fact, if your idea has potential and you choose to collaborate with us we'll invest in you through royalties of your work. We believe that our success comes from inspiring people to learn and share as they discover the world.

We therefore work to encourage a participatory culture that provides opportunities to share individual's works on a global scale. We distribute our products and services internationally every day and we feel that exposure adds value to individuals' credibility and reputations. As we help you to build your resume and reputation you'll be able to network with many talented people who are also seeking to share themselves, build their portfolios, and contribute to something more than themselves. We believe that everyone is creative and has something to offer. That's why we want you to ask yourself; how you want to be remembered? We hope that you will enjoy sharing with us and we are pleased to be able to invest in you.

Who are the proud creators of the World Voice Project?

The World Voice Project Book Series presents an opportunity to become a part of one of the largest emerging Community Learning Networks (CLN) of human socio-cultural expression and inclusive global experience. The stories shared here allow people to explore their world through the eyes and experiences of another while adding to the historical record of these times. What we share with each other helps to create the understandings necessary to weaken the injustice and ignorance that causes so much pain in our lives. This project seeks to build an honest solidarity amongst people and to foster unity amongst global individuals.

As Santiago Inc. grows, we will attempt to surround ourselves with those people who inspire us. We believe progress is reliant on those people interested in making a difference in their world. Therefore we strive to attract those who will join us in our efforts to the capacity they are able and we thank those of you who are already making a contribution. We are a community within your community. In sharing what truly matters to you, you will learn that you are not alone. So whether you're a buyer or a contributor to the World Voice project or Santiago Inc., we hope you'll recognize yourself as the change you want to see in this world. Share your voice!
Check it out .Worldvoiceproject.com

We don't exist without you!

On behalf of Santiago Inc. we thank you for taking the time to learn a little about us. If you would like to volunteer to help on a project or wish to do an internship please contact us and tell us about your interests. Thank you for supporting us!

Joseph A Santiago, President, Santiago, Inc.
JosephS@Santiago-inc.com